short AND simple

FAMILY RECIPES

short AND simple

FAMILY RECIPES

·

Amy Roloff

WITH **Chris Cardamone**

PHOTOGRAPHY BY **Rick Schafer**

WestWinds Press®

*To my family and kids and all the
friends who come to my home.*

Library of Congress Cataloging-in-Publication Data

Roloff, Amy.
Short and simple family recipes / Amy Roloff with Chris Cardamone.
    p. cm.
   ISBN 978-0-88240-888-0 (pbk.)
1. Quick and easy cooking. 2. Cooking, American. I. Cardamone, Chris. II. Title.
TX833.5.R653 2012
641.5′55—dc23

2012016667

WestWinds Press®
An imprint of Graphic Arts Books
P.O. Box 56118
Portland, OR 97238-6118
(503) 254-5591

www.graphicartsbooks.com

Designer: Aimee Genter-Gilmore

A portion of the proceeds from the sale of this book will
go to the Amy Roloff Charity Foundation.

Printed in China

acknowledgments

Thank you, Mom and Dad, for allowing me to see the world and discover the one thing that helped me be a part of it. My parents, Gordon and Pat Knight, gave me the love and community of family. There was no better place where I felt more togetherness than around the family dinner table enjoying a wonderful meal and talking about all sorts of topics. I can't thank my mom and dad enough for letting me explore and be creative in the kitchen with food throughout my childhood because it helped me become the person I am today. I fell in love with food and cooking because of their encouragement and support to do what I so enjoy: cooking and bringing people together. It's all about family.

I want to thank Chris Cardamone for recognizing the desire I had to do something more with my love of cooking after he heard about a dream I had. His knowledge of food and cooking was an inspiration to me, and he encouraged and pushed me for a long time to just go ahead and do it: gather all of those recipes I'd used over the years and write a book. Without his friendship, input, and encouragement, this book might not have happened at this time.

I also want to thank Rick Schafer, my food photographer for his support. Sometimes a chance meeting can lead to something really worthwhile, fun, and exciting. I love to cook, but Rick helped me see the creative side of food and presentation even more. His pictures of the recipes I prepared made even me say, "Wow!"

I want to thank my family for letting their mom and wife turn the family kitchen into a place where I could be creative, test recipes on them, and where people love to gather around the table to share a meal because my kids insist that "My mom is the best cook ever" and "I'd rather have one of my mom's meals than go out to eat or eat at anyone else's house." Ah, sweet music to my ears! The recipes are short and simple but the memories of our meals together are long and last a lifetime.

—Amy J. Roloff

contents

CHAPTER 3: LIGHT LUNCH FARE

CHAPTER 4: TIME TO GATHER

CHAPTER 5: SWEET ENDINGS

foreword

We all dream. We dream of many things; climbing the mountain that we see from our kitchen window, or maybe visiting exotic far- away countries. Sometimes we dream about the things we could do when we win the grand lotto. These dreams are like wisps of smoke rising from a smoldering campfire, they cross our minds, and then they are set aside, with the thought, maybe, just maybe tomorrow I'll climb that mountain or visit that faraway country. Amy has had many dreams, but there is a dream that had its beginnings when she was a young girl in her teens. "Someday I'm going to own my own restaurant, or maybe a B&B, and write a book—a cookbook." These were some of Amy's dreams that would not leave her. Even though for many years they had lain dormant in the distant regions of her mind, the dreams were always there.

Though there was no real planning on Amy's part, the experience and practical hands-on involvement of planning and preparing a meal were, in a way, dropped upon her at a very early period in her life. Each of Amy's two older sisters had the responsibility of preparing the evening meal. As they moved on to other activities outside of the family, Amy was given both the opportunity and daunting responsibility to plan and prepare the family's evening meal. We had certain apprehensions as to whether Amy would be capable of meeting the challenges, keeping in mind that Amy was a little person. Her chin touched the top of the kitchen counter, she was practically eye level with the stove, and the knobs were in the back, and most everything she needed, like the sink and water, dishes, and many of the ingredients to cook with, were out of her reach. She needed several step stools to assist her in cooking.

Amy surprised us all and quickly adapted to the kitchen, and she overcame the physical challenges. After all, the world was not changing just because she was a little person. At the beginning of Amy's culinary experience, the evening meals were very basic. As she became more aware of food, ingredients, and the kitchen, her creativity began to show in not only what she cooked but how she served the dish. Amy would pore over our cookbooks and cooking magazines, and they became part of the décor of the kitchen counter and table. We can remember tasting some of the meals she made at the very beginning, and let's just say, the food didn't move.

We gladly agreed to be the guinea pigs as she defiantly experimented with recipes. They were edible, but she often needed to go back to the kitchen and try again. That she would do. Amy would try again and again, revising some of the recipes to suit her palate and requirements: keep it short, simple, and tasty. Amy's desire to cook and prepare dinner was very much appreciated by both of us.

Early on, a local TV station heard about Amy being a little person in a family of average-size parents and siblings and asked if they could film a short segment titled, "A Day in the Life of a Little Person." The program included cooking the evening meal for the family. Something happened after that. The experience of showing her life on TV was the awakening of her new found forte and the beginning of her culinary journey.

We were thrilled that Amy found something she loved doing. As our family kitchen became her kitchen, she not only grew as a person, but also her cooking became more tantalizing. Amy took us all by surprise with her enthusiasm and desire to cook every night. She wasn't modifying packaged dinners; she was creating homemade family meals we all enjoyed together at the dinner table. As her mother went to work and ended up finding something she enjoyed doing, Amy not only found what she loved doing, she also was a huge help to the family. We were appreciative of Amy and the help she gave to us, and her siblings were pretty thrilled too. We kept our tradition and the importance of family dinners and sharing with each other every night. We were not surprised that, in college, one of her desired majors was hospitality.

As you read through the various sections of this book, you will realize that Amy has created a cookbook that represents years of practice and time poring over recipes for the family. Preparing meals for a family of four siblings and her parents on a daily basis, with a limited budget and within a limited time frame, requires organization and knowing about ingredients and how, when combined, they will taste and be enjoyed by her family and guests.

This cookbook, *Short and Simple Family Recipes*, has been a labor of love and commitment. We know that when the recipes are tried, the results will be both gratifying to the cook and pleasing to your family.

—Gordon and Pat Knight,
Amy's parents

introduction

IT'S JUST LITTLE OLD ME, AMY!

Waking up early in the morning has always been special to me. There is something inspiring about watching the sun crest the horizon to welcome the adventures of the day. I love the smell of a strong pot of coffee brewing as I wait for the rest of the world to wake up around me. I'm not sure what it is that compels me, but I have to cook or bake something every morning. Don't get me wrong, it's not just about breakfast; it's about all foods with big, delicious flavors that make your taste buds dance. That is what I dream about. As a "cooking mom" for four ravenous kids, I am an equal-opportunity enjoyer when it comes to food. Morning, noon, and night, I am drawn to the kitchen.

On the topic of breakfast, blueberry and lemon come to mind—two of my favorite flavors. Inside this cookbook you'll find my coveted blueberry muffin recipe: scrumptious, warm, and subtle. Bring it together with a bursting crunchy sugary lemon top. Like most things in a house with four kids, these muffins don't last long. As a mom, there is nothing better than making something tasty, satisfying, and fresh for your children to devour before they head off for a busy day. It means the most to me. I welcome you into everything I love: to my recipes, my life, and my family. But enough about that . . .

At a young age, I was indelibly marked with a love of food and the sensory adventures it entails. I quickly realized, thanks to the aromas wafting from my childhood kitchen, that food and I would become friends. Enticing smells of herbs, spices, and sweets filled our kitchen and waltzed through our small house in Michigan. Those early memories beckoned me to pursue food as an agent to bring those I love together. Also, in some small way, it stripped away some of my own personal insecurities.

What was this magic that great meals had to gather everyone together? I needed to have whatever this power was that food had over people to create lasting memories. I wanted to cook!

I grew up in a small, nondescript home in suburban Michigan. We could have afforded a bigger house, but my father was practical, and the house was enough for us. It was ground zero for me and shaped almost everything about who I am today. It is where I learned the value of family and that I was different from other kids. It is also where I fell in love with food.

I watched, smelled, and tasted as my mother made family dinners and entertained for special events. To say I was shy is an understatement. However, when my parents hosted dinner or a party, the food was the center of attention: not me being different. I appreciated the shift in focus and was utterly drawn in by food and how it created such magical bonds between people. It was an easer of tensions and builder of communions; I loved it and longed to conjure such feelings when I cooked. As time went by, I found myself cooking more and more. As a little person, others would have to help me cook, but the disadvantage and challenge never thwarted my passion. Being different from others was engrained in my mind from the beginning. However, when I cooked and people truly enjoyed what I created, all those feelings fluttered away. I was just like them. Simply and honestly, I love to cook.

Being different, cooking was one way for me to level the playing field. As I maneuvered through the kitchen, up and down on step stools, I knew I could make the same things anyone else could. My best memories as a kid centered around food, family, and friends. When the conversation was electric around the table, and when the smiles seemed endless just because of what I

whipped up in the kitchen, I was hooked and in love with making good food.

Who knew making Christmas cookies as a girl would lead me down a path dedicated to good food and great times with those I love? Gathering ingredients, making the measurements exact, the smells and sizzles of cooking, and watching all those elements magically come together into a tasty dish for others is thrilling every time. As I cooked more and more, I thought, "Wow, cooking is exciting and makes me feel like I belong here." Regardless of being little, I was proud to share what I made with my family and friends. Strangely enough, I discovered a different acceptance of myself, because everyone, for the most part, loved what I cooked. To me, accepting my food meant accepting me.

My father and mother both worked to give my siblings and me a better life. My mom worked late and would return home to the burden of making dinner for all six of us. The burden of two jobs—provider and mother—started to take its toll. One day, my father asked me if I wanted to start making dinner for the family. He said it would help alleviate the stress of cooking on my mother. With my passion for cooking, I said yes! I couldn't wait to unlock more of its hidden treasures and treats. I didn't see the responsibility of cooking for my family as a chore. I looked forward to it. Suddenly, I found myself as the Knight family chef. I welcomed the request, and the rest is history. On most days I would rush home from school, finish my homework in a blur, scavenge cooking magazines for new ideas, then race to the kitchen to start dinner. By no means was I good, but through trial and a lot of error, I started to get more and more

confident in the kitchen—and that confidence was all mine.

I enjoyed every facet of being the family chef, especially the time it gave me with my father, Gordon. I looked forward to trips to the local grocery store with my dad. The market gave off smells and a seemingly endless array of possibilities. I was overwhelmed by the varieties of dishes and meals I could prepare with what the store had to offer. So many possibilities, and I was dying to make all of them! I created my own shopping lists. Even if my father was skeptical about my combinations, he bought the ingredients every time. His doubt wasn't unfounded. My father's pride and trust in my budding culinary skills were tested from the start as he muscled through many of my most inedible concoctions. Regardless of how awful a recipe was, my dad was a champ, and so was the rest of the family. They ate whatever crazy thing I put in front of them. Looking back, I will always cherish those supermarket trips and my family's gracious intestinal courage.

My family was on the front lines of my culinary disasters and successes, and for that I thank them. Even back then, much like now, I never willingly feed my family processed, pre-packaged meals. In this book you will not find many (if any) processed foods or pre-packaged meals. They have too many chemicals and too much salt. These foods belong in a science lab, not on the dinner table. Food just tastes a whole heck of a lot better and is better for you when it's made and shared fresh with family and friends.

My love for food and entertaining didn't end at home as a girl. Entering college, I enrolled as a hospitality major with a focus on the food and beverage industry. After getting my degree, I was passed over many times in the industry because of my short stature. The most important thing I learned in college was acceptance thanks to a group of friends I still talk to today. You think food was involved?

I made many friends in college. One night, a group of my closest friends were shipping off to the military, and it would be the last time I saw them for a while. This was the perfect time for me to flex my little culinary muscles and make a great meal to send my friends off in style, and maybe with a few lasting memories. It wasn't anything special. I think I made oven-fried chicken, garlic potatoes, asparagus, and apple pie. We ate, we worried, we reminisced, and we hoped that someday we would all be back together again. By the night's end, this special meal had brought us together just before the realities of adulthood would break us apart. It was an epic night. I realized that sharing food with those I care about would be a meaningful and indelible part of the rest of my life. It's funny how just thinking about my recipes for oven-fried chicken takes me back so many years. It makes me remember the importance of good food and how it brings people together.

I took so much from that dinner that made me realize how important food also is to being a family. As a mom, I have continued my love of cooking and use it to spend time with my kids. Every night, my kids know that mom is cooking. They know something tasty is on the way, and I secretly know it's my time to catch up with them and maybe weigh in on the tribulations of their days. Food encompasses not only my kids and family but also their friends and their families. Anyone who knows me knows there is always room for one more at dinner. The most sacred part of my life as a cook is making simple, healthy meals that gather those I love around a table. Heck, sometimes we eat standing up in the kitchen, but I wouldn't trade those moments for anything.

Those moments are my life. Those moments are my memory. I welcome and encourage you to share the same experience. My heart melts seeing my kids chow down on something I've whipped up and then say, "Mom, there is nothing like your cooking." I went from a shy, different little girl who never thought she had a chance to do anything big in this world to a mother of four. I cherish every moment we are together, and food is the conduit. I never thought I would be as fortunate as I am, and cooking for my family is the cherry on top. I remember every spaghetti soccer dinner, every homemade birthday cake, every Thanksgiving and Christmas dinner with my kids. Food is like my mental scrapbook. Those moments will last forever. I hope the recipes I have in this book create lasting memories for you and those you love.

This cookbook has been in the making for years. I started and stopped, started and stopped forever. I began this literary cookbook adventure because I wanted to share my love of food, family, and those special moments with you. The journey happened for two reasons: to spread the special acceptance cooking gave me and teach others how to build bonds between those you love using food. Over the years, viewers have watched me cook on the show *Little People, Big World*. Many fans ended up reaching out to me to ask for recipes they saw

me make on the show. Along the way, the many viewer recipe requests piled up. One day, I realized something: people liked watching me cook just as much as they related to seeing a family sit down to dinner together. The realization spoke to my heart and to two things that mean a lot to me—family and mealtime.

As, what I will term, a "kitchen-mom" who cooks even with a busy schedule, making food for my family has always been a top priority. Mealtime or dinnertime (time set aside to eat together as a family) in our fast-paced age is something that is withering away. My hope is that, together, you and I will bring family mealtime back because it means so much. To me, there is nothing more important than spending time with family and feeding them well. I cherish all fifteen or more minutes when my kids and family convene around the dinner table on a nightly basis. Regardless of how much time I put into cooking, with hopes of keeping everyone at the table, the fifteen minutes sharing time as a family is worth every moment.

Bring cooking and family time back. Not by buying it, but by cooking it! Spend the time to show those you love that you care. Spend the time teaching those you love how to cook and make healthy, satisfying foods together. Bring *real* food back and make lasting memories along the way. That's it. That's all. Short and simple. Trust me, I know the memories you create will fill you up for a lifetime as they have for me. This book is a big part of me; I hope I have stirred up a little part of you. Welcome to my family.

—Amy J. Roloff

pantry essentials

The word "pantry" is deceptive. To me it means two things: a closet with dried foods and those things that last forever in my fridge. Both are key! The kitchen "pantry" is your friend. Not an area where you have a lot of stuff and ingredients you don't know about. You have to have a relationship with your pantry without asking yourself, what is this and is this stale? Your pantry should complement you, how you cook, what you cook, and provide some surprises and creativity. I think of my pantry as my lifeline in the kitchen.

As a kid I remember our kitchen pantry stocked full, packed, and organized. Although I am uncertain, I think my mother was worried we'd run out of something, so we always had every kind of rice, condiments, sauces, potatoes, sugar, flour, and more package dinners than you could imagine. As a teenager, the one thing that called to me was our pantry and the limitless options provided by the ingredients I found there. The pantry became my canvas. Each critical ingredient was another color for my palette. I call my pantry my paint box.

There are a number of key pantry essentials I like to have on hand. You choose your own list, but these are my must-haves:

Breads:
- French bread
- White bread

Wine:
- Pinot noir
- Cabernet
- Zinfandel
- Chardonnay
- Pinot gris

Rice:
- Jasmine
- Brown
- Basmati

Potatoes/Squash:
- Russet potatoes
- Red potatoes
- Yukon gold potatoes
- Red baby potatoes
- Sweet potatoes
- Butternut squash
- Spaghetti squash

Pasta/Grains:
- Spaghetti
- Penne
- Linguini
- Fettuccine
- Elbow
- Quinoa

Oils/Vinegar:
- Extra-virgin olive oil
- Canola oil
- Sesame oil
- Red wine vinegar
- Apple cider vinegar
- Balsamic vinegar

Canned/Jar Foods:
- Tuna fish
- Crabmeat
- Pinto and black beans
- Corn
- Green chilies
- Tomato sauce
- Diced tomatoes

- Tomato paste
- Sun-dried tomatoes
- Marinara sauce
- Pesto sauce
- Low-sodium chicken and beef broth
- Black olives
- Pineapple
- Pears
- Apple sauce
- Cherry, blueberry, raspberry fillings
- Pumpkin filling
- Cranberries
- Condensed and evaporated milk

Baking:
- All-purpose flour
- Cake flour
- Cornmeal
- Bread crumbs—regular and panko
- Sugar—brown and granulated
- Baking soda
- Baking powder
- Cornstarch
- Unsweetened chocolate
- Semisweet chocolate
- Cocoa powder
- Vanilla
- Coconut, sweetened and shredded
- Lemon extract
- Almond extract
- Peppermint extract

Dried Fruits/Nuts:
- Cranberries
- Apricots
- Raisins
- Whole and slivered almonds
- Pecans
- Walnuts
- Sesame seeds
- Flax seeds
- Pumpkin seeds
- Sunflower seeds

Condiments:
- BBQ sauce
- Ketchup
- Relish
- Mustard—Dijon and brown
- Maple syrup
- Honey
- Soy sauce
- Worcestershire sauce
- Salsa
- Peanut butter
- Jams
- Powdered milk
- Cooking spray
- Tabasco or other hot sauce

Dried spices/herbs:
- Cinnamon—ground and sticks
- Allspice
- Nutmeg—ground and whole
- Ginger
- Cloves—ground and whole
- Cardamom
- Cumin
- Chili powder
- Garlic powder
- Italian seasoning
- Basil
- Sage
- Thyme
- Bay leaf
- Oregano
- Rosemary
- Salt—kosher and sea salt
- Ground pepper and whole pepper
- Cayenne pepper
- Chipotle seasoning
- Paprika
- Dill weed

The above pretty much covers what I love to have on hand so when we have a snowstorm or the electricity goes out I'm set. Our generator will give me enough light and power to prepare a great meal by candlelight.

As for refrigerator, freezer, and fresh essentials, I think it varies depending on what you like to cook on a daily basis. I prefer fresh for most things, especially herbs, but sometimes that isn't always possible. I get what I think I will need for the next few days or week.

Freezer:
- Frozen fruits
- Frozen vegetables
- Frozen fish
- Frozen shrimp
- Boneless chicken breast
- Pork loins
- Ground hamburger and sausage
- Beef roast

Refrigerator:
- Lemons
- Limes
- Oranges
- Apples—Red Delicious and Granny Smith
- Green onions
- Cilantro
- Parsley
- Cucumber
- Radishes
- Romaine
- Arugula
- Carrots
- Celery
- Sweet yellow onions
- Light sour cream
- Low-fat cream cheese
- Low-fat whipping cream
- 2 percent milk
- Variety of cheeses
- Shredded cheese
- Butter
- Extra-large eggs
- Bacon
- Pancetta
- Bell peppers
- Garlic

FOR starters

I like to casually entertain by having friends over for a charity function, holiday, special occasion, or to welcome new guests to my home. Starters are a wonderful way to begin your evening and set the stage for the whole night. I prefer not to spend hours in the kitchen making appetizers, because I want to visit and spend time with friends and guests. The starters in *Short and Simple Family Recipes* are tasty, quick, and say to your guests, "I'm glad you're here!"

Growing up, I don't remember my folks entertaining often. And I think my mom thought she would rather spend time on the main course instead of appetizers. She also knew my aunt would handle the appetizers anyway. My sisters, brother, and I loved the holidays because of my aunt's appetizers and desserts. I remember as I got older, my folks played cards and pinochle with three other couples they had known for years. That is when I discovered my mom was pretty clever with her appetizers. I loved their once-a-month card night at the house. My sisters, brother, and I would sneak into the kitchen to pilfer some of the appetizers mom made. It was like we had our own little party, too. Sometimes we would "volunteer" to help pass them around so we could sneak samples. I also noticed that appetizers set the mood for the evening. The enjoyment I saw and heard with laughter and good conversation coming from the living room gave me another perspective on how food brings people together and creates memories.

Now, my kids do what I did as a kid. When I have good friends over, host parties, or charity events in my home, the kids know mom always makes more than needed. I have a fear of running out of food, so they know they can sneak appetizers all night long. They call friends to come on over because I had "made treats" and they would get the leftovers. Sometimes they make a meal just out of the starters! I don't mind, because it's my house, my kids, and my people.

The starters in this cookbook are simple, tasty, and will make your party an enjoyable event without you spending a day in the kitchen or causing you to miss out on your own party.

flat bread pizza

ingredients

1 head garlic

Olive oil

Kosher salt and pepper

3 Roma tomatoes

1 package fresh low-fat mozzarella

1 (15-ounce) can diced tomatoes

1 (15-ounce) can tomato paste

2 tablespoons minced fresh garlic

2 teaspoons dried Italian seasoning

8 ounces Brie cheese

4 ounces low-fat cream cheese

1 teaspoon dried Italian seasoning

2 premade pizza crusts (or use fresh
   pizza dough)

1 cup fresh roughly chopped basil

½ cup Parmesan cheese

> " *This recipe is quick and easy. It makes a great snack for kids, too. I love garlic, so unless you're getting close with someone, put on as much as you want. You can add different herbs and cheeses depending on what you like. Molly loves this simple pizza because it involves cheese and bread. Jacob loves it because it's pizza. When I invite company over they enjoy the casual elegance and scrumptious taste because it gives them the OK to have pizza.* "

This is a basic pizza appetizer recipe. I have listed two of my favorite toppings for the pizzas. It is quick and always a crowd pleaser.

Preheat oven to 400°F. Slice about ¼- to ½-inch off the top of the garlic head. Cut a piece of foil to about 12 inches by 12 inches. Place foil in the bottom of an oven-safe sauté pan or dish and add garlic head cut-side up, drizzle with olive oil and sprinkle with kosher salt and pepper. Wrap garlic with foil and put in oven to roast for 40 minutes. (I check on the garlic every 10 to 15 minutes because when the cloves get translucent and brown your roasted garlic is done.)

Wash and slice Roma tomatoes and slice the mozzarella; set aside. In a blender, puree the diced tomatoes, tomato paste, fresh garlic, and 2 teaspoons Italian seasoning. Add salt and pepper to taste and set aside.

Cut Brie into 1-inch pieces; do the same with cream cheese. Put Brie and cream cheese into microwave-safe bowl. Add roasted garlic and 1 teaspoon Italian seasoning. Microwave Brie mixture three times for about 30 seconds each time to soften. Remove and blend all ingredients until smooth and completely combined.

Adjust oven temperature to 425°F. Place two pizza dough rounds on pizza pans. Spread tomato sauce topping on one. Layer with sliced tomatoes, mozzarella, and basil. On the second pizza, spread Brie mixture and top with Parmesan cheese. Bake for 10 to 15 minutes until the cheese melts. Remove and cut with a pizza cutter into squares. Enjoy!

Serves 6 to 8

savory shrimp & cherry tomato

WITH CUCUMBER DIP

ingredients

24 large shrimp, uncooked
Salt and pepper, to taste
1 tablespoon minced garlic
1 teaspoon olive oil
¼ teaspoon chili powder
½ lime, zested and juiced
2 tablespoons olive oil
12 cherry tomatoes, halved
Cocktail toothpicks

Cucumber Dip:
1 cup low-fat Greek yogurt
1 teaspoon minced garlic
1 teaspoon lemon zest
½ teaspoon lemon juice
½ teaspoon coriander
½ teaspoon red pepper flakes
1 tablespoon chopped cilantro
1 English cucumber, finely chopped
Salt and pepper, to taste
Fresh cilantro, for garnish

Remove skin and tails from shrimp and devein. In a medium bowl, mix together shrimp, salt and pepper, garlic, 1 teaspoon olive oil, chili powder, and lime zest and juice. Stir and set aside.

In a small bowl, combine yogurt, garlic, lemon zest and juice, coriander, red pepper flakes, and chopped cilantro. Mix in cucumber, add salt and pepper to taste, and set aside.

Heat 2 tablespoons olive oil in a large sauté pan; add shrimp and sauté until pink, about 2 to 3 minutes per side. Don't crowd or overcook shrimp. If your shrimp are large, you may need to cook in two batches. Place a halved cherry tomato and shrimp on each toothpick. Arrange on plate next to cucumber dip. Garnish with fresh cilantro. Enjoy!

Serves 12

mushroom
goat cheese puffs

ingredients

Olive oil

1 tablespoon minced fresh garlic

1 small yellow onion, thinly sliced

Approximately 20 cremini mushrooms
  (or your favorite), sliced

2 tablespoons butter

6 ounces goat cheese

Salt and pepper, to taste

1 package puff pastry, thawed

1 egg white, slightly beaten

Preheat oven to 425°F.

Heat a large sauté pan to medium high and drizzle with 2 tablespoons of olive oil. Add garlic and sliced onion, cooking until onions caramelize to a golden brown color, about 4 minutes. Add sliced mushrooms and sauté for another 3 to 5 minutes. Add butter to the pan with goat cheese, reduce heat, and sauté another 2 minutes until butter and cheese have melted and are combined. Add a dash of salt and pepper. Remove from heat and set aside.

Dust flour on to your cutting board. Unfold puff pastry on top of the floured surface. Smooth out puff pastry so it is of even thickness and cut into approximate 3-inch squares.

Spray a baking sheet with nonstick spray. Place puff pastry squares on the baking sheet. Spoon approximately one tablespoon of the mushroom goat cheese mixture into the center of each square. Fold opposite corners of puff pastry and pinch together. Don't worry if corners pop open; it looks great when cheese and mushroom oozes out. Brush the top of each pastry with a little beaten egg white. Bake until puff pastry is golden and flaky, about 15 to 20 minutes. Makes 12 to 18 puffs. Enjoy!

Serves 6 to 8

party meatballs

Sauce:

Olive oil

1 tablespoon minced garlic

1 cup tomato sauce

1 cup orange marmalade

¼ cup chili sauce

¼ cup brown sugar

1 orange, zested and juiced

2 tablespoons red wine vinegar

1 tablespoon Worcestershire sauce

¼ teaspoon red pepper flakes

Salt and pepper

Meatballs:

1 pound 94 percent lean ground beef

1 small shallot, minced

½ cup panko bread crumbs

½ cup Parmesan cheese

½ teaspoon fresh thyme (or 1 teaspoon dried thyme)

1 large egg, beaten

1 tablespoon chopped flat-leaf parsley

2 tablespoons buttermilk

1 teaspoon salt

1 teaspoon pepper

Cocktail toothpicks

Preheat oven to 400°F. For sauce, heat a large sauté pan over medium high. Drizzle a little olive oil, add garlic, and sauté for about 1 minute. Now add tomato sauce, marmalade, chili sauce, brown sugar, orange zest and juice, red wine vinegar, Worcestershire sauce, and red pepper flakes. Stir with a whisk to combine completely. Simmer for about 10 minutes. Add salt and pepper to taste. Remove from heat and prepare meatballs.

In a large bowl combine ground beef, minced shallot, bread crumbs, Parmesan cheese, thyme, beaten egg, parsley, buttermilk, salt, and pepper. Using your hands combine all meatball ingredients. Now shape meatball mixture into ping-pong size meatballs. Place on baking sheet. Bake until almost done, about 15 minutes. Remove from oven and gently incorporate meatballs into sauce mix. Cook on medium high for another 15 minutes. Skewer meatballs with toothpicks and place on a serving platter. Makes about 12 to 18 meatballs depending on how large you make them. Enjoy!

Serves 8 to 10

quesadillas any style

ingredients

8 large tortillas, flour or whole wheat

Olive oil

Salsa filling:

½ cup fresh salsa, or quality store-bought

4 Roma tomatoes, diced

¼ cup finely chopped yellow onion

1 jalapeño pepper, seeded and finely
   chopped

Salt and pepper

1 tablespoon minced garlic

½ teaspoon chili powder

1 lime, zested and juiced

½ cup partly mashed black beans

2 cups shredded Cheddar or mozzarella
   cheese

¼ cup chopped fresh cilantro

Pear filling:

3 to 4 pears, thinly sliced

1 tablespoon brown sugar

¼ cup thinly sliced toasted almonds

¼ pound Brie cheese, thinly sliced

¼ cup crumbled blue cheese

½ cup chopped fresh cilantro

Here are two quick recipes I've used for appetizers that are completely different in flavor. Feel free to use your creative culinary imagination and come up with your own combos.

In a medium bowl, add salsa, diced Roma tomatoes, yellow onion, jalapeño, a dash of salt and pepper, garlic, chili powder, lime juice, and lime zest. Stir to combine and set aside.

Heat medium sauté pan to medium high and drizzle lightly with olive oil. Place one tortilla in the pan. Spread half of the tortilla with one-fourth of the salsa mixture, and the other half with one-fourth of the black beans. Sprinkle with one-fourth of the cheese and cilantro. Now fold tortilla in half. Reduce heat to medium and allow the cheese to melt; flip to brown both sides. When the cheese is melted remove from the pan, cool for about a minute, and then cut into 4 triangles. Serve warm.

Here is another version I like. Thinly slice pears and place in bowl with brown sugar, toss to coat and set aside. Toast almonds in a sauté pan over medium heat until golden, stirring often to ensure they don't burn. Remove from heat and set aside.

Heat a medium sauté pan to medium high and drizzle with olive oil. Add tortilla. Next, place one-fourth of the thinly sliced Brie, crumbled blue cheese, sliced pears and brown sugar mixture, and chopped cilantro on top of tortilla. Fold in half. Reduce heat to medium to allow the cheese to melt, then flip to brown both sides. When the cheese is melted remove quesadilla from the pan, cool for about a minute, and then cut into 4 triangles. Serve warm. Enjoy!

Serves 8

scallop pesto crostini

ingredients

12 to 18 large sea scallops,
   fresh or previously frozen
Olive oil
1 tablespoon minced garlic
Salt and pepper
1 or 2 loaves French bread

½ cup pesto sauce, homemade (see
   recipe *pg. 65*) or fresh from a store
½ cup light mild salsa
Parmesan cheese, fresh shavings or
   store-bought, grated
Fresh chives, chopped

Preheat oven to 425°F.

In a medium bowl, add scallops, a drizzle of olive oil, garlic, salt and pepper, and toss lightly to coat. Heat a medium skillet on high with 1 tablespoon of olive oil. Add scallops and cook until slightly browned on both sides. Remove from heat and keep warm in pan.

Slice French bread into ½-inch slices. Place sliced bread on baking sheet and toast lightly in oven for about 5 minutes. On each bread slice, spread a couple teaspoons of pesto sauce and mild salsa. Place a scallop on each piece with sprinkling of Parmesan cheese shavings and chives. Place in oven for about 5 minutes until heated thoroughly, remove, and place on platter.

Season with salt and pepper to taste. Enjoy!

Serves 12 to 18

> " *I made this recipe for a wrap-up party I was having with our TV crew. I didn't have much time to make a lot of appetizers but wanted to serve something that wasn't premade. I knew seafood would not only be quick, but special too. Preparing scallops is easy and doesn't take a lot of time.* "

crab cakes

½ cup frozen green peas

2 cups fresh lump crabmeat (or high
   quality canned crabmeat)

1 lemon, zested and juiced

4 tablespoons chopped chives

4 tablespoons chopped yellow onion

¼ cup chopped carrots

Salt and pepper, to taste

½ cup, plus 2 tablespoons low-fat
   Greek yogurt

Dash Tabasco sauce

1 egg, slightly beaten

¼ cup panko bread crumbs

4 tablespoons Parmesan cheese

Nonstick cooking spray

1 jar (about 4 ounces) chopped pimentos
   with liquid

¼ teaspoon crushed red pepper
   flakes

1 bunch of baby arugula

Heat oven to broil. Place peas in small microwave bowl and heat for 1 minute. In another large bowl combine crabmeat, lemon zest and juice, chopped chives, yellow onion, carrots, salt and pepper, and peas. Stir to combine.

Now add ½ cup of yogurt, Tabasco sauce, slightly beaten egg, bread crumbs, and cheese. Mix all ingredients with a fork until combined and dough forms. Pat dough into 6 crab cakes, or smaller if you want bite-sized crab cakes. Lightly spray baking sheet with nonstick cooking spray. Place cakes on prepared baking sheet and broil for about 6 minutes on each side.

In the meantime, combine chopped pimentos and liquid, remaining yogurt, and crushed red pepper flakes in blender. Pulse until combined, and then season with salt and pepper to taste. Toss arugula with a little of this dressing, reserving the rest, and place crab cakes on top. Then drizzle cakes with remaining dressing. Enjoy!

Serves 6

baked potato slices

ingredients

8 red potatoes

Olive oil

Salt and pepper, to taste

6 to 8 slices bacon

½ cup low-fat sour cream

2 tablespoons chopped chives (reserve some for garnish)

¼ cup shredded Cheddar cheese

Heat oven to 425°F. Wash potatoes and remove any blemishes. Cut potatoes into thick slices, about ¼ inch, 4 to 5 slices per potato, and discard the ends.

Place potatoes slices on baking sheet and drizzle with olive oil. Sprinkle with salt and pepper. Roast for about 15 to 20 minutes until tender but not mushy.

Meanwhile, heat a medium sauté pan to medium high and render bacon until crispy. Remove bacon and drain on paper towel to cool. After cooled, crumble bacon into a small bowl and set aside. In a separate small bowl, add sour cream, half the chives, and stir to combine.

Remove potatoes from oven. Dollop sour cream chive mixture on top of each potato slice, and add about ¼ teaspoon of bacon crumbles and shredded cheese. Place back in oven until cheese slightly melts, about 3 minutes. Remove from oven and garnish with chives. Using a spatula arrange potato slices on a serving platter. Makes about 24 to 30 slices. Feel free to add other toppings that you might desire. Enjoy!

Serves 10 to 12

breakfast OR brunch

Growing up in Michigan, I was always told by my mother ". . . breakfast is the most important meal of the day." It took me awhile, but my mother was right. It's true! There is something about the start of a new day and a tummy filled with good food. Maybe it's just my anticipation of the day's adventures, or the freshness of food, or the aromas of sweet and salty blending together that gets me so excited. In this chapter you'll find quick breakfast and brunch recipes that need little time to prepare—and ones to splurge on when you have time to spare on a weekend. Either way, breakfast or brunch is a bright way to say, "Good morning!"

My dad would always be the first up brewing coffee and cutting up fresh fruit. In our house fruit was put on top of hot cereal or in homemade pancakes. Sometimes I'd get up early with him, sneak some fruit to put on top of yogurt and make fresh muffins. What a wonderful way to begin the day and prepare for whatever's ahead. My dad often told me, "You'd better eat now because you never know when you'll eat again." Eating with the family was his special way of saying he was glad to start the day with his loved ones.

I have come to love being the first one up in the morning, whether it's cloudy, rainy, or the sun is brightly shining. Today, as the coffee brews, I wonder when to wake the rest of my family so we can attack a busy school day, work, errands, business meetings, charity work, or meetings with friends. A great way I found to get my kids up and ready is to bake fresh blueberry muffins, or make yogurt topped with granola and fruit drizzled with maple syrup. Sometimes it's my omelet in a pan served with toasted French bread, or cowboy eggs. In this chapter you'll find my family breakfast favorites and brunch recipes and much more. Even though cold cereal with fruit is every busy mom's faithful companion, I've added a few quick on-the-go recipes for when the alarm clock doesn't go off. Yikes!

And one last thing: breakfast isn't just for mornings. Breakfast is an anytime-of-day meal for me. During college and my early days of raising a family, breakfast recipes saved me. There is something about having breakfast for dinner that just says goodness! My kids get excited when I say, "Pancakes and bacon for dinner." Or when we whip up bagels with salmon, cream cheese, tomato, and dill—or sauté up a heap of leftover hash browns with ham for dinner. Who knew breakfast could be something to enjoy any time of day. When it's late, you're hungry, and just want a little something, breakfast is the solution. Maybe it's French toast with crusty French bread topped with Bananas Foster to end the day. A good breakfast can get your day started right, or provide the perfect ending to a busy day.

Seize the day, or night!

baguette french toast

WITH FRESH JAM

ingredients

1 French baguette, day-old is best

4 eggs

½ cup half and half

½ teaspoon ground cinnamon

½ teaspoon pure vanilla extract

1 teaspoon granulated sugar

1 cup heavy whipping cream

2 tablespoons powdered sugar

1 cup fresh preserves (your preference)

2 tablespoons cooking fat

Fresh cut fruit—bananas and strawberries

(or any other combo you prefer)

With a sharp bread knife, cut baguette on the bias (angle to make French toast slices bigger). Set aside—it's okay if the bread gets dried out. Crack the eggs into a shallow baking dish, then whisk to break them up. Add half and half, cinnamon, vanilla, and sugar. Set aside.

In a mixer, whip whipping cream with powdered sugar until soft peaks form. Measure out preserves and put into a small serving dish with a knife or spoon.

I love making this special French toast before church for something to really look forward to when we come home. A very special twist to French toast is to make it for brunch. To keep my kids in the groove of waking up at a decent time on Saturday during the school year, the smell of French toast and sweet fruit often does the trick. Sometimes it's a special breakfast to make when company comes over. My family loves any morning when toasty homemade French toast is served.

Heat large skillet or sauté pan to medium high heat. When the pan or skillet is hot, add 2 tablespoons of bacon drippings (this is what I prefer), canola oil, or butter. Dip two or more slices of baguette into the egg mixture, coating both sides. Place coated baguette slices in pan to cook. Brown each side for about 2 minutes. Repeat with remaining slices.

To serve, place one or two pieces of baguette French toast on a plate, then spread with preserves and the strawberry and banana mixture. Top with fresh whipped cream. Enjoy!

Serves 4 to 6

breakfast OR anytime crumb cake

ingredients

Topping:

1 cup dark brown sugar, packed

¼ cup sugar

1½ tablespoons ground cinnamon

½ teaspoon salt

1 cup (2 sticks) unsalted butter, melted and warm

2 cups all-purpose flour

1 cup chopped toasted pecans, optional

Cake:

2½ cups all-purpose flour

1 teaspoon baking soda

2 teaspoons baking powder

½ teaspoon salt

¾ cup (1½ sticks) unsalted butter, melted but kept warm

1¼ cups sugar

2 large eggs, room temperature

1⅓ cups sour cream

1 teaspoon vanilla

Mix both sugars, cinnamon, and salt in medium bowl, stirring to combine. Add warm melted butter and stir until blended. Add flour and mix with fork until moist clumps form. Stir in pecans if desired. Mixture will look slightly wet. Set aside.

Position rack in center of oven and preheat to 350°F. Grease a 9 x 13-inch glass baking dish with either cooking spray or rub vegetable shortening on bottom and sides of dish and dust with flour. Sift flour, baking soda, baking powder, and salt into a medium bowl.

In a large bowl, use electric mixer to cream butter. Add sugar and beat until light and fluffy. Add eggs, one at a time, beating until well blended, and scrape the sides of the bowl after each addition. Add sour cream and vanilla extract and beat just until blended. Add flour mixture in 3 additions, beating until just incorporated. Transfer cake batter to prepared baking dish; spread batter evenly with rubber spatula. Sprinkle topping evenly over cake batter, covering completely, and use your hands to press it down slightly.

Bake for 45 to 50 minutes or until toothpick inserted into the center comes out clean and the top is golden brown. Cool cake in dish on rack for about 30 minutes before slicing. Serve warm or at room temperature with fresh fruit and coffee. Enjoy!

Serves 8 to 12

cowboy eggs

ingredients

4 pieces Texas-style bread

¼ cup butter

4 eggs

8 slices bacon (or deli ham)

½ cup mild salsa

Shredded Cheddar cheese

4 slices cantaloupe

Strawberries

Heat a large skillet or sauté pan over medium high heat. On a cutting board, lay out the pieces of bread, and using a small glass or biscuit cutter about 2 inches in diameter, cut out the center of the bread and set aside. Repeat for the three remaining slices of bread.

Preheat oven to 425°F. Place 8 slices of bacon in a baking pan in the oven. Cook for about 15 minutes until the bacon is done but not too crispy.

With the skillet hot, add a small amount of butter or cooking spray, and coat the pan. Lay the bread with centers removed into the pan. Flip bread after one side is toasted and crack an egg into the center of the bread. Put center pieces that were set aside in the skillet to toast and brown. Allow eggs to cook and reduce heat.

When eggs firm up a bit, flip toast/egg over and brown the other side. Once eggs are firm (if you prefer softer yoke you don't need to flip over), remove from skillet and place on plate. Serve cowboy eggs with the centerpiece on top and a little salsa and Cheddar cheese on top of the toast. Add 2 slices of cooked bacon, a slice of cantaloupe, and fresh strawberries on the side. Enjoy!

Serves 4

This is the boys' favorite. This simple version came from watching a cooking show with my dad and Matt. It has everything—eggs, bacon, thick Texas-style toast—and it's easy and quick. I call them cowboy eggs for that very reason and everything is served together. Zachary is into history and this breakfast dish reminds him of being on the cowboy trail. Try these when you are hungry and need a good quick meal and don't have a ton of prep time. If you are rushing around getting ready for school or work, cowboy eggs fits the bill in my house.

blueberry muffins

ingredients

Butter or nonstick cooking spray
½ cup sugar
1 lemon, zested and juiced
¼ cup sugar
½ teaspoon pure vanilla extract
1½ sticks unsalted butter, room temperature
⅔ cup sugar
½ cup brown sugar, packed
3 extra-large eggs, room temperature

1½ teaspoons pure vanilla extract
1 cup sour cream
¼ cup milk
2½ cups all-purpose flour
3 teaspoons baking powder
½ teaspoon baking soda
½ teaspoon salt
2 cups blueberries, fresh or frozen

Spray muffin cups with nonstick cooking spray or rub with butter. Add sugar to each cup and rotate pan to coat inside with sugar, then set aside. Put the lemon zest into a small bowl. Add lemon juice, sugar, and vanilla. Combine and set aside.

In a large electric mixer bowl, cream butter and both sugars with paddle attachment until light and fluffy, about 5 minutes. With the mixer on low speed, add one egg at a time, scraping the sides of bowl after each egg. Beat until fluffy. On low, add vanilla, sour cream, and milk. In a separate bowl sift together flour, baking powder, baking soda, and salt.

With the mixer still on low, add flour mixture to batter and beat until just combined. Fold in blueberries with a spatula and be sure the batter is completely mixed. (If berries are frozen, thaw and drain excess liquid before adding). Put batter in fridge for about 30 minutes to set.

Preheat the oven to 375°F. Pour batter into the prepared muffin cups, filling each cup ¾ of the way to top. Put a teaspoon of the lemon zest mixture on top of each muffin cup, and use a knife to make a figure 8 with the tip of the blade. Place muffins in oven and bake for about 25 to 30 minutes, or until muffins are lightly browned on top. The muffins are done when a knife or toothpick inserted into the center comes out clean. Enjoy!

Makes 24 muffins

> " *I modified a recipe when we grew our own blueberries. My family loves blueberries and eats them like candy. They are so good, versatile, and what better way to have them than in warm, sweet muffins. The blueberries and a hint of lemon zest make these muffins disappear before they have had a chance to cool down! When I want to make something special for breakfast without some of the other breakfast fixings, these muffins go over well with my kids.* "

scrambled eggs
WITH SPINACH, HAM, & CHEESE

ingredients

8 large eggs

¼ cup milk

Salt and pepper, to taste

1 green onion, finely chopped

1 teaspoon minced garlic

2 cups roughly torn spinach

6 slices deli ham, torn

½ cup shredded cheese, reserve
   ¼ cup for garnish

Butter or nonstick cooking spray

Paprika

Crack the eggs into a large mixing bowl and whisk until broken up. Now add milk, salt, pepper, chopped green onion, and garlic. With your whisk, beat until combined. Add the torn spinach, ham, and ¼ cup of cheese. Again with your whisk, beat to combine.

Heat a large sauté pan over medium heat. Add a pat of butter or spray the sauté pan with nonstick cooking spray. Once the pan is heated, pour in the egg mixture.

Stir often to scramble the eggs. Cook until done, depending on your taste, firm or slightly wet. Sprinkle remaining cheese and a pinch of paprika over the eggs. Serve with a side of toast. Enjoy!

Serves 4

berry pancakes
WITH MIXED BERRY SYRUP

ingredients

3 cups all-purpose flour

4 teaspoons baking powder

1½ teaspoons baking soda

3 tablespoons sugar

Dash salt

2 cups low-fat milk

3 eggs

4 tablespoons butter, melted (or canola oil)

2 cups frozen mixed berries, thawed

1 cup frozen raspberries, thawed

Butter, for pan

Fresh berries for garnish

Powdered sugar

For the syrup:

2½ cups sugar

1 cup corn syrup

½ cup apple juice

½ teaspoon vanilla

½ teaspoon ground cinnamon

2 cups frozen blueberries

1 cup frozen mixed berries

Prepare berry syrup first, before pancake batter, as it will need time to reduce and thicken. In a nonstick medium saucepan combine sugar, corn syrup, apple juice, vanilla, and cinnamon. Turn up to high heat, bring the mixture to a boil, and then reduce heat. Add 2 cups frozen blueberries and 1 cup frozen mixed berries to the sugar mixture, stirring to coat.Bring syrup mixture up to a boil again, then reduce heat to a simmer. Allow berries to break down and the syrup to thicken. After simmering for 20 minutes, remove from heat and set aside to cool. You can leave the berries whole in the syrup or blend them up, your choice. Once cooled, pour berry syrup into a blender and puree for a minute. Pour berry mixture into a fine strainer to remove the seeds.

 One of my oldest sons, Zachary, would be happy for life if he had pancakes every morning. These are extra special with fruit, and so, my Molly is one happy camper too. It's always a great Saturday morning when you wake up to the smell of pancakes and fresh berry syrup.

For pancakes, lay out paper towels on a cookie sheet. Spread thawed frozen berries on paper towels to remove excess water.

In a large bowl, sift together flour, baking powder, and baking soda. Mix in sugar and salt to flour mixture. Whisk in milk and eggs, then whisk in melted butter and beat until batter is fluffy and thick. Fold thawed berries into pancake batter.

Heat a large skillet or sauté pan to medium high heat. Melt about 1 tablespoon of butter in pan or spray with nonstick cooking spray. Use a ½-cup measure or a large serving spoon to pour the pancake batter into the pan. Flip when bubbles form on top and the bottom is golden. Repeat until all pancakes are made. Plate pancakes and serve with berry syrup, fresh berries, and powdered sugar. Enjoy!

Serves 6

farm country omelet

1 tablespoon olive oil

1 cup roughly chopped Yukon gold or red potatoes

Salt and freshly ground pepper

6 to 8 large eggs

4 tablespoons milk

¼ to ½ cup finely grated Swiss or Cheddar cheese

1 tablespoon unsalted butter

6 precooked breakfast sausages, sliced (or bacon if preferred)

1 tablespoon chopped fresh chives

Preheat oven to 375°F. Heat an ovenproof medium sauté pan over medium heat and add olive oil. Place potatoes in pan and sprinkle with salt and pepper. Continue to cook over medium heat for about 10 minutes until browned and just tender but not mushy.

In medium bowl, whisk eggs, milk, and ¼ cup of cheese. Add butter to the sauté pan, then add egg mixture and cooked sausages. Cook for about 3 minutes over medium heat, then remove from stove top. Finish cooking the omelet by placing the pan into oven for another 5 minutes, or until cooked and firm throughout. Try not to overcook or omelet may be tough. Sprinkle the top with remaining cheese and chives. Cool for 2 minutes then remove from the pan. Slice like a pie and serve with fruit and good hearty bread. Enjoy!

Serves 2 to 4

granola bars FROM SCRATCH

ingredients

2 cups old-fashioned oats (not quick oats)
1 cup slivered almonds
½ cup pumpkin seeds (or sunflower seeds)
1 cup shredded coconut
½ cup flax seeds
3 tablespoons butter
⅔ cup honey

¼ cup corn syrup
¼ cup light brown sugar
2 teaspoons pure vanilla extract
½ cup raisins
½ cup dried cranberries
½ cup chopped dried apricots

Preheat oven to 375°F. Grease an 8 by 12-inch baking pan and line it with parchment or wax paper. This will help when cutting the granola into bars and prevent sticking.

Combine oats, almonds, pumpkin seeds, and coconut together on baking sheet. Use your hands to combine. Bake for 10 to 15 minutes, stirring occasionally, until all the ingredients are lightly browned. Transfer mixture to large mixing bowl and mix in flax seeds.

Reduce oven temperature to 300°F. Place butter, honey, corn syrup, brown sugar, and vanilla in a small saucepan and bring to a boil over medium heat. Cook and stir for about 2 minutes until all ingredients are dissolved. Remove from stove and pour over toasted oat mixture. Add the dried fruit and stir well.

Pour mixture into prepared baking sheet pan with parchment paper. Wet or grease fingers and gently press the mixture evenly into the pan being sure not to press too hard.

Bake for 25 to 30 minutes until lightly browned. Cool for 2 to 3 hours before cutting into squares. If some of the mixture crumbles away, save for a crunchy topping over baked fruit, ice cream, cobbler, oatmeal, or yogurt. Enjoy!

Makes 16 to 20 bars

great start smoothie

ingredients

2 ripe bananas

2 cups unsweetened strawberries, fresh (or slightly thawed frozen ones)

1 cup crushed ice

½ cup orange juice

½ cup low-fat milk

1 cup plain low-fat yogurt

¼ cup honey

½ teaspoon pure vanilla extract

This is simple. Combine all ingredients in a blender. I start with the fruit on the bottom, add the ice, and then the juices and liquids. This makes for a better smoothie because depending on the strength of your blender it can struggle with the ice at the bottom. Pulse blender at the start, then run on high until all ingredients are combined.

If you run into problems, pulse your blender or rock it back and forth to loosen up your smoothie mixture. Enjoy!

Variations:

Use blueberries, raspberries, blackberries, mango, kiwi, dried cherries, etc.

Serves 1

" *There are so many different varieties of smoothies. Fresh smoothies are a great, quick start for a busy morning. Use the fresh or frozen fruit of your choice, yogurt, and you can even add wheat germ and almonds for extra crunchy goodness. Molly loves fruit and makes smoothies all the time, especially during the summer. My kids prefer to get creative and mix and match tons of different fruit in their smoothies. You should do the same!* "

lemon scones

WITH HOMEMADE BLACKBERRY JAM

Scones:

2 cups flour

4 teaspoons baking powder

½ teaspoon salt

4 tablespoons sugar

6 tablespoons butter, ice cold from freezer

1 egg, slightly beaten

¾ cup cream, plus more for brushing

1 teaspoon lemon zest

1 teaspoon lemon juice

Granulated sugar (for dusting)

Homemade blackberry jam:

1 tablespoon butter

3 cups frozen or fresh blackberries

¼ cup sugar

½ teaspoon lemon zest

½ teaspoon lemon juice

Dash nutmeg

1 teaspoon pectin

For the scones:

Preheat oven to 400°F. In a large bowl, mix the flour, baking powder, salt, and sugar, stirring to combine. Chop frozen butter into chunks, then with a pastry blender or fork cut butter into dry ingredients until mixture resembles beach sand. In a medium bowl, whisk egg and cream until blended. Add lemon zest and juice to dry ingredients along with egg/cream mixture. Mix until just moistened. Flour hands and knead dough on a floured surface until the dough comes together. With a rolling pin, roll dough into a rectangle to about ¾ inch thick. Cut dough into triangle shapes, about 8. Brush or sprinkle tops with cream and dust with a little sugar. Bake for about 20 minutes until browned. Serve with butter and homemade jam. Enjoy!

For the jam:

Heat a medium saucepan over medium heat to melt butter. Stir in blackberries, sugar, zest, juice, and nutmeg. Mash berries with spoon or potato masher. Slowly bring to a low rolling boil. Stir in pectin and continue on low rolling boil until thickened for about 5 minutes. Pour into a small serving bowl to cool and let set for about a ½ hour. You can store this in airtight containers in the refrigerator.

Makes 8

breakfast wraps

ingredients

8 large eggs

4 wheat tortillas

4 large red-leaf lettuce leaves

1 avocado, pitted, peeled, and sliced

1 medium tomato, sliced

1 red pepper, thinly sliced

¼ cup shredded provolone or Swiss cheese

1 tablespoon hot sauce

Olive oil

½ teaspoon salt

½ teaspoon freshly ground pepper

Place eggs in medium saucepan and cover with water. Bring water to a boil then reduce heat and simmer for 10 minutes. Remove from heat, rinse with cold water, and peel eggs.

Preheat oven to 350°F.

Slice up hard-boiled eggs, then set aside. Put tortillas in microwave and sprinkle with a little water. Microwave for 45 seconds to make them pliable. Remove and place lettuce leaf in the center of each wrap, top with avocado, hard-boiled eggs, tomato, red pepper, and cheese. Sprinkle with hot sauce, olive oil, and salt and pepper. Fold one side of wrap over the filling to form a pocket and roll into a wrap. Place wrap on a baking sheet and into the oven to heat and melt cheese, 5 to 7 minutes. Eat them now, or cover in foil and store in refrigerator for up to a day. Serve with seasonal fruit. Enjoy!

Serves 4

> " *This is quick, especially if you already have hard-boiled eggs in the fridge. Most of my kids love avocado, but if they don't, I either leave out or substitute with sliced cucumbers. You can change this up and put some of your favorite items in the wrap and make it your own.* "

oatmeal
WITH APPLES & BROWN SUGAR

1 cup water

2 cups low-fat milk

Dash salt

2 cups old-fashioned oats, not instant oatmeal

½ cup chopped walnuts, (or your favorite nut)

1 apple, your favorite variety; sliced and chopped, reserve some for garnish

½ cup brown sugar

½ teaspoon cinnamon

Heat water, milk, and salt in a medium saucepan, slowly bringing to a boil. Pour in oats. Stir while still at a rolling boil for about 1 minute, then reduce and simmer for 15 to 20 minutes.

Toast walnuts in small sauté pan for 3 to 4 minutes and remove to cool. In a small bowl, combine nuts, chopped apples, brown sugar, and cinnamon. Toss to coat. Add apple mixture to oats and stir to combine completely, reserving a little for garnish.

Divide oatmeal into four bowls and garnish with reserved apple mixture. Pour cream or milk over top. Enjoy!

Serves 4

hot chocolate mix

ingredients

6 cups powdered milk

3 cups powdered sugar

1½ cups cocoa powder, at least 30 percent cacao

4 cups nondairy creamer

1 teaspoon cinnamon

½ teaspoon salt

1 pound dark chocolate, shaved

In a large mixing bowl, combine powdered milk, powdered sugar, cocoa powder, nondairy creamer, cinnamon, and salt together. With a fine cheese grater shave dark chocolate into the bowl. Mix dark grated chocolate into dry mixture and combine completely.

Store mix in an airtight container.

To make cocoa:

In a mug, add 1 cup of hot water to 4 large teaspoons of cocoa mix. Stir well.

Note:

You can add whatever you want to spice up this cocoa mix—a dash of cayenne pepper, nutmeg, cardamom, mints, or even dried berries chopped up fine. Enjoy!

Makes about 40 servings

 When the weather cools down and fall is in the air, Jacob loves making and drinking hot chocolate. I make sure I have plenty of mini marshmallows on hand, too. It's great to have this hot cocoa mix ready to go for when you crave chocolate. You can also package it up and give it as a gift.

light lunch fare

As a kid, I always prepared homemade lunches with my mom. As I got older and started making food for myself, I realized I learned from the best. Even when I wanted to do the cool thing and get "hot lunch" at school, to tell you the truth, I liked my mom's touch in making sandwiches better. I remember leftover meatloaf sandwich, a salad, and the different kinds of bread she used, and, of course, my name on the bag.

I remember my mom would buy the freshest produce. The light bulb went off in my head that buying fresh and local was the way to go. I have fond memories of going to the grocery store with my dad, with him ensuring that I put the healthy items in the cart. Lunchmeats, treats, fruits, and chips were all things I wanted in my lunch bag.

These Lunch Fare recipes offer a variety of ideas for anytime in the afternoon. Turkey soup to warm you up on a dreary day, grilled panini sandwiches instead of simple grilled cheese, and a tuna fish sandwich to remind you that a lazy beach day isn't far away. For my family, lunch happens at school and as a light snack before soccer practice.

> *I rarely ever buy premade burgers. Homemade burgers are always better. Each one is specially made, and the little time is worth it. My kids love these burgers because it's like having a party when I make them. It's an easy, quick meal, especially when friends are around. The flavors are more than enough, but you can add whatever condiments you want. I always have barbecue sauce on hand for Jacob. My kids especially like burgers when it's cold outside. Warm meat and a toasty bun are a little piece of summer during rainy Oregon winters.*

super burgers WITH GARLIC FRIES

Burgers:

3 pounds 94 percent lean ground beef

1 egg

1 teaspoon each, salt and pepper

1 tablespoon minced garlic

½ cup Parmesan cheese

1 teaspoon Italian seasoning

Fries:

1 package frozen French fries

½ cup canola oil

2 tablespoons minced garlic

Salt and pepper, to taste

1 teaspoon Italian seasoning

Condiments:

Cheddar cheese slices

Romaine hearts, washed and flattened

Roma tomatoes, sliced

Kosher pickle slices

Yellow onion, sliced into rings

Avocado, sliced

Bacon, cooked and drained

Jalapeño pepper slices

Mustard

Ketchup

Barbecue sauce

Mayonnaise

Hamburger buns, toasted

For the burgers:

In a large mixing bowl, add ground beef, egg, salt and pepper, garlic, Parmesan cheese, and Italian seasoning. Mix to combine. Make large, meatball-sized portions of meat, rolling them in your palms until tight and compact. With both hands, pat the meatball into a saucer shape. Line a plate with foil or plastic wrap. Set formed hamburger patties onto it. Repeat with hamburger mix until all patties are done.

Heat grill or large sauté pan. If using a sauté pan, sprinkle a dash of salt into the bottom of the pan. Grill or sauté burgers until they reach your desired state of doneness.

For the fries:

What are burgers without fries? Preheat the oven following instructions on bag of French fries. In a large bowl, empty the bag of fries, add canola oil, garlic, salt, pepper, and Italian seasoning. Toss fries to coat completely. Spread out fries on baking sheet, and bake. Halfway through the required cooking time, toss fries around to ensure they get crispy and golden on all sides. Remove from oven and serve hot.

The most fun part of burgers is the condiments. You want an array of condiments to offer your guests so they can build their burger to their taste. Get a large serving platter and lay out cheese, romaine hearts, sliced tomatoes, pickles, sliced onions, avocado, cooked bacon, and jalapeño pepper. Set out mustard, ketchup, barbecue sauce, and mayonnaise. And don't forget to set out knives. Enjoy!

Note: For homemade garlicky fries, see recipe on page 100.

Serves 12

tuna fish sandwiches

ingredients

2 large cans albacore white tuna (or whatever you prefer)

⅓ cup light mayonnaise

3 tablespoons Dijon mustard

2 green onions, thinly sliced, optional

½ teaspoon fresh dill (or 1 teaspoon dried)

½ teaspoon paprika

Salt and pepper, to taste

4 tablespoons sweet relish

1 dash hot sauce

4 slices wheat bread, toasted

Leaf lettuce (or arugula)

I have to say, this is Matt's favorite lunch or anytime sandwich. He is the King of Tuna Fish. If he could, Matt would eat all of it in one sitting. Lettuce and tomatoes go great with this sandwich. If you want to make that old-time favorite, Tuna Melt, add real Cheddar cheese and melt in the oven. Put oven on broil and heat until cheese melts. Another variety he likes is with just a little relish and lots of mustard—that's it. Simple.

Open and drain tuna fish cans. Empty tuna into a medium mixing bowl, add mayonnaise, mustard, sliced green onion (if using), dill, paprika, salt and pepper, relish, and hot sauce. Toast bread in toaster or oven until golden brown.

If desired, on each slice of bread spread mayonnaise or mustard, spread about 4 tablespoons tuna fish on one half, add lettuce, then top with other half of bread. Cut in half. Serve with your favorite side. Enjoy!

Serves 2

roast beef sandwiches
WITH ZESTY HORSERADISH

ingredients

2 Roma tomatoes sliced

½ small red onion, thinly sliced

8 slices Swiss or provolone cheese

French baguette

1 small bunch arugula, stems removed

1 tablespoon Italian dressing, store-bought

24 ounces lean deli roast beef, thinly sliced

Zesty horseradish:

⅓ cup plain yogurt

4 tablespoons mayonnaise

3 tablespoons shaved horseradish, store-bought, excess juice, drained

1 tablespoon Dijon mustard

½ lemon, zested

½ teaspoon salt

½ teaspoon pepper

To make the horseradish, remove liquid from yogurt with a strainer or other method until thick. This will take about 15 minutes. In a small bowl, combine yogurt, mayonnaise, horseradish, Dijon mustard, lemon zest, salt and pepper. Whisk together until combined. Cover, and allow to rest in fridge for 20 minutes.

Preheat oven to 425°F. Prepare sandwich condiments. On cutting board slice Roma tomatoes, red onion, and cut Swiss cheese slices into halves. Cut baguette into 4 pieces, each piece approximately 6 to 8 inches long. Slice each baguette in half lengthwise. Lay out 8 slices of baguette on a baking sheet; cut-side up. Toast in oven for 2 minutes. Remove and set aside.

In a medium bowl, toss arugula leaves with a little Italian dressing. Remove horseradish spread from fridge. Build each sandwich with 2 pieces of bread, one with cheese and one without. Place 2 slices of Swiss cheese on each of 4 baguette pieces. Return to the oven until cheese is melted. Remove and slather 2 tablespoons of horseradish spread on each of the 8 baguette pieces. To the cheese side, add 2 slices of tomato and 2 slices of onion. To the non-cheese side, add a small amount of dressed arugula greens. Now add 6 ounces of roast beef and put the 2 pieces of baguette together. Cut the sandwich in half and serve with your favorite chips or fries. Enjoy!

Serves 4

When I don't have time or am not in the mood to cook a big dinner, this is a great substitute. My kids love to have these sandwiches. I like making this before or after I come home from the boys soccer games or Molly's volleyball games. This sandwich is flavorful and packs a zing with the horseradish and Dijon.

ham, cheese, & turkey avocado panini

ingredients

¼ cup low-fat mayonnaise

1 tablespoon relish

1 teaspoon ketchup

Salt and pepper, to taste

½ teaspoon Dijon mustard

¼ cup low-fat mayonnaise

¼ teaspoon chili powder

4 slices hearty ciabatta bread

Deli ham slices

Cheddar cheese

Arugula, optional

Olive oil

Deli turkey slices

Provolone cheese

1 avocado, thinly sliced

In a small bowl, combine mayonnaise, relish, ketchup, salt and pepper, and Dijon mustard, mix, and set aside. In second small bowl, combine another ¼ cup mayonnaise and chili powder, mix to combine, then set aside.

On one slice of bread spread mayonnaise relish mixture, lay on deli ham, Cheddar cheese, and arugula. Place second piece of bread on top, brush with olive oil, and press in oiled panini grill. Cook until toasted brown and cheese melts. Slice diagonally. If you don't have a panini grill, use two medium sauté pans instead—using one to cook panini and the other one on top to provide pressure during cooking on the stove top.

For the other two slices of bread, spread the bottom slice with mayonnaise–chili powder mixture, deli turkey meat, provolone cheese, sliced avocado, and top with arugula. Place second piece of bread on top, brush with olive oil, and press in panini grill. Cook until brown and the cheese melts.

Feel free to add onions if desired or change up depending on your taste. This is what my kids like. Enjoy!

Serves 2

chicken cobb salad
WITH CITRUS CILANTRO DRESSING

ingredients

2 large heads romaine lettuce
2 ears fresh corn, grilled or steamed,
    and kernelled
½ pound bacon
Black and green olives, sliced
¾ cup shredded pepper jack cheese
2 chicken breasts, previously cooked,
    (see Simple Chicken recipe, *pg. 52*)
4 hard-boiled eggs, peeled
Roma tomatoes
1 avocado, pitted
4 slices baguette

Dressing:
1 lime, zested
3 limes and 2 lemons, juiced
½ bunch green onion, thinly sliced
1 teaspoon sugar
3 teaspoons garlic
2 teaspoons cumin
1 bunch fresh cilantro
1 cup olive oil
Salt and pepper

For the salad:

Wash and remove romaine's outer leaves, then tear hearts into a large salad bowl. Add kernel corn to the salad with romaine. Cook the bacon and drain on paper towels, then crumble into salad. Add olives and shredded cheese. Cut chicken breasts into slices or cubes, then set aside. Slice eggs, Roma tomatoes, avocado, and set aside.

This is one of the dinner salads my kids and family love. We have it in late spring and the summer months, but any time works. Chicken is one of Jacob's favorite meats so he doesn't hesitate to eat this and get his veggies too. I like it because it's fresh and I love cilantro on anything!

For the dressing:

In a small bowl, combine lime zest and lime and lemon juices. Now add green onion, sugar, garlic, and cumin. Whisk together. Roughly chop cilantro and add to the dressing base. Whisk continuously while streaming in olive oil until the dressing emulsifies. Add salt and pepper to taste. Pour dressing on top of salad and toss to coat. Arrange dressed salad on several plates.

Place the chicken in the center, and then fan out hard-boiled egg, Roma tomato, and avocado slices on three sides of the plate. Serve with baguette slices. Enjoy!

Serves 4

bold greek salad

1 medium, ripe tomato

Handful of cherry tomatoes

1 beefsteak or heirloom tomato

½ large red onion, thinly sliced and
    quartered

2 large English cucumbers, seeded,
    thickly sliced

1 yellow bell pepper, seeded and sliced

¾ cup kalamata olives, slightly crushed
    with hands to remove pit

8-ounce block feta cheese, not crumbled

1 heaping tablespoon oregano

Dressing:

¼ cup red wine vinegar

1 tablespoon minced garlic

1 teaspoon sea salt

½ teaspoon ground pepper

6 sprigs fresh dill, roughly cut

½ lemon, zested

1 lemon, juiced

¼ teaspoon balsamic vinegar

½ cup extra-virgin olive oil
    (or your favorite brand)

De-seed and slice ripe tomato into medium chunks, cut cherry tomatoes in half, then slice up heirloom tomato and cut slices in half. Place all tomatoes and red onion in a large salad bowl.

Run the tines of a fork down the sides of the cucumber to score, cut in half, and remove seeds with a spoon. Cut cucumber up in chunks and then place in bowl with tomatoes. Add yellow bell pepper and olives. Roll block of feta cheese in oregano, then cut up cheese into chunks and add to other ingredients.

For the dressing, in a small bowl whisk red wine vinegar, garlic, salt, pepper, dill, lemon zest, lemon juice, balsamic vinegar, and olive oil together. Pour dressing over salad, making sure to toss and coat. Let sit for about 30 minutes in the fridge so flavors develop. Serve with crusty bread or toast points. Enjoy!

Serves 6

southwestern slaw

ingredients

1 cup corn
½ head small green cabbage
½ head small red cabbage
1 red bell pepper
1 cup black beans
2 Roma tomatoes, diced
2 green onions, sliced
1 bunch cilantro, roughly chopped
2 pre-cooked chicken breasts, see
   Simple Chicken recipe (*pg. 52*)

Dressing:
1 teaspoon minced garlic
2 limes, juiced
1 lime, zested
1 teaspoon chili powder
½ teaspoon cumin powder
¼ teaspoon chipotle seasoning
1 tablespoon olive oil
Salt and pepper, to taste

Preheat oven to 425°F. Place corn on baking sheet, and roast for 10 to 15 minutes. Remove and set aside.

Slice and shred red and green cabbage and place in a large microwave-safe bowl. Sprinkle water on cabbage and microwave for about 1 to 2 minutes. (This eliminates the raw cabbage taste.)

Seed and thinly slice the red bell pepper. Add roasted corn, bell pepper, black beans, tomatoes, green onion, and cilantro to cabbage.

In a small bowl, mix garlic, lime juice, lime zest, chili powder, cumin powder, chipotle seasoning, and olive oil. Pour dressing over salad, and toss to coat. Slice chicken breasts and add to slaw. Season to taste with salt and pepper. Transfer salad to a large serving bowl. Garnish with cilantro sprigs.

Serve with pita or tortilla chips. Enjoy!

Serves 8 to 10

fresh fruit salad

ingredients

1 small seedless watermelon, cubed

1 cantaloupe, seeds removed and cubed

4 kiwi, peeled and cut into ½-inch-thick
slices, then halved

2 cups fresh raspberries

2 cups fresh blackberries

2 cups blueberries

4 cups hulled and sliced fresh strawberries

1 pineapple, peeled, cored, and cubed

4 Pippin apples, peeled, cored, and cubed,
tossed with 1 tablespoon
lemon juice to stop discoloration

½ cup orange juice

½ teaspoon pure vanilla extract

1 tablespoon granulated sugar

¼ cup chopped fresh mint leaves

> " *A great light salad all summer long. This is Molly's favorite—as always she is obsessed with fresh fruit. I take the time to make the salad because she loves it and it tastes like summer. Wonderful to make a few hours ahead so the fruit has time to mingle together and mix flavors. If you use bananas add them last so they keep their color and do not get mushy. A complement to anything you have made for a summer meal.* "

In a large bowl, combine watermelon, cantaloupe, kiwi, raspberries, blackberries, blueberries, strawberries, pineapple, and apples.

In a small bowl combine orange juice, vanilla, and sugar, then whisk together. Chop up mint and add to mixture. Pour the juice and mint mixture over the fruit. Toss to coat. Serve in chilled bowls with a plain rye cracker. Enjoy! For the fall season, try apples, pears, grapes, oranges, and bananas with a hint of cloves.

Serves 12

blt salad

ingredients

2 large heads romaine lettuce
2 to 3 Roma tomatoes, chopped
4 slices red onion
¼ cup brown sugar
1 teaspoon paprika
1 lemon, zested
1 teaspoon ground pepper
3 sprigs fresh thyme
6 to 8 thick bacon slices

Croutons:
6 large slices French bread
Olive oil
Dash salt and pepper
Garlic powder, optional

Dressing:
½ cup low-fat mayonnaise
2 tablespoons maple syrup
2 teaspoons whole grain brown mustard
1 tablespoon lemon juice
Salt and pepper

Preheat oven to 375°F.

For the salad, wash and remove romaine's outer leaves, then tear hearts into a large salad bowl. Add tomatoes and red onion.

In a separate bowl combine brown sugar, paprika, lemon zest, pepper, and thyme. Press bacon slices into mixture. Lay flat in baking sheet and bake until caramelized and crispy, about 20 minutes. Let cool, and then cut into bite-sized pieces and set aside.

For the croutons, cut bread into cubes and toss in baking pan with olive oil, salt and pepper, and garlic powder. Toast until golden brown and crunchy in oven. Let cool.

For the dressing, combine mayonnaise, maple syrup, mustard, lemon juice, salt, and pepper in a small bowl and whisk to combine.

Toss bacon in salad, add dressing, and toss to coat. Top with croutons. Serve with good, hearty bread. Enjoy!

Serves 6

quiche lorraine

ingredients

1 pie crust, premade or homemade

8 slices bacon

½ teaspoon olive oil

½ cup finely chopped onion

1 cup fresh mushrooms

1½ cups shredded Swiss cheese

4 eggs, slightly beaten

1 cup light half and half

1½ cups whipping cream

½ teaspoon salt

Dash salt and pepper

Dash nutmeg

When my kids were younger, we'd sometimes sleep in on Sunday mornings, and they always enjoyed it when we had a quiche brunch. It was truly a special day when we got to hang out, have fun, and enjoy breakfast together. I really like making this anytime, but especially during the spring, Easter, and summer months. It's a light meal and goes well with a green leaf salad, fruit, crusty bread, or muffins. It's brunch time!

Preheat oven to 400°F. Bake pie crust for 7 minutes. Remove from oven, and set aside to cool.

Reduce oven temp to 375°F. In a large skillet, cook bacon until crisp and then crumble it; set aside. Heat a small sauté pan on high, add olive oil, onions, and mushrooms, and sauté for 1 to 2 minutes. Set aside.

Into pie crust, sprinkle cheese first, then bacon, then onions and mushrooms.

In medium bowl, beat eggs, half and half, whipping cream, salt, pepper, and nutmeg. Pour egg mixture into pie crust. Shake pan to get out bubbles, then bake for 50 to 55 minutes, or until knife inserted comes out clean. Let stand for about 10 minutes. Serve with fresh fruit or crispy toast. Enjoy!

Serves 4 to 6

hearty turkey soup

ingredients

1 large sweet yellow onion, roughly chopped

3 large carrots, roughly chopped

3 celery stalks, roughly chopped

4 tablespoons olive oil

Salt and pepper, to taste

1 teaspoon dried sage

1 teaspoon dried thyme

1 teaspoon dried rosemary

1 turkey carcass—if leftover turkey
    carcass not available, then use: 1 pound
    cooked turkey meat, shredded or cubed,
    white and dark meat

2 cups vegetable stock

2 bay leaves

1 tablespoon peppercorns

1 lemon, zested

Preheat oven to 400°F.

In a medium bowl, toss chopped onion, carrots, and celery with olive oil and a dash of salt. Put the veggies into a roasting pan and add sage, thyme, and rosemary. Roast veggies until slightly browned, about 20 to 25 minutes.

In a large stockpot, add turkey carcass, vegetable stock, bay leaves, peppercorns, and lemon zest. Fill the pot with water to cover carcass and place on stove. Turn heat to high and bring to a boil. Boil for about 1 hour and cover the pot. After an hour reduce the heat to a simmer or low boil, then cook for 30 more minutes to create a turkey broth. If using turkey meat instead of carcass, omit water and use vegetable broth that contains herb seasonings. Simmer for about 15 minutes and follow remaining directions.

Remove from heat and allow to cool. Remove any remnants of the turkey carcass. Add roasted veggies and return to stove over medium heat until flavors come together. If desired add your favorite pasta or rice. Enjoy!

Serves 6 to 8

This is another way I enjoy using leftover turkey carcass and meat. Our family likes making 'the turkey' last a little bit longer. I love making this soup because it's warm comfort food on a cold fall or winter day. I make more than what we can normally eat. That way when I'm working on a project or running to a charity event there is still good food my kids can heat up to have a healthy, satisfying meal.

shrimp salad
WITH QUINOA & ARUGULA

ingredients

3 tablespoons salt

½ lemon, cut into 4 slices

2 pounds large shrimp in the shell (about 16 to 20 per pound)

½ cup light mayonnaise

¼ cup light sour cream

½ teaspoon Dijon mustard

1 tablespoon white wine (or white wine vinegar)

2 tablespoons minced fresh dill

½ teaspoon each salt and pepper

¼ cup minced shallots (about 2)

1 avocado, roughly chopped

1 cup minced celery (3 stalks)

Quinoa:

2 cups chicken stock

1 cup quinoa, dry

1 teaspoon olive oil

Salt and pepper, to taste

2 tablespoons roughly chopped fresh parsley

12 grape or cherry tomatoes, cut in half

½ tablespoon minced garlic

Bunch of arugula

Bring 2 quarts of water to a boil in a large saucepan. Add salt and lemon slices and boil. Add half the shrimp and reduce the heat to medium. Cook uncovered for about 3 minutes or until shrimp are barely cooked. You don't want to overcook them or they'll be tough and chewy. Remove with slotted spoon into a bowl of cold water to stop cooking. Bring water to a boil again and cook remaining shrimp. Let cool, then devein and peel shrimp. Set aside.

In a separate small bowl, whisk together mayonnaise, sour cream, mustard, wine or vinegar, dill, salt, and pepper. Combine with the peeled shrimp. Add minced shallots, avocado, and celery. Add salt and pepper to taste. Cover and refrigerate for about 30 minutes.

In a medium saucepan, bring chicken stock to a boil and add quinoa with 1 teaspoon of olive oil. Add salt and pepper to quinoa. Cook according to quinoa box directions. Once quinoa is cooked, add parsley, halved tomatoes, and minced garlic. Salt and pepper to taste.

To serve, place a portion of quinoa on a plate, top with a handful of arugula then top with shrimp salad. Serve with crusty bread. Enjoy!

Serves 4 to 6

time TO gather

My first attempt at cooking started with dinners. I watched my mother over the years in wonderment asking myself how does she know what to do? What ingredients? How much time? The result of her labors was almost always a delicious meal we all enjoyed around the family table. Dinnertime was very important in my family, and the kids knew we needed to be there and that all of us wanted to be together. The talks and stories my father told always had a message for me. He was always teaching and had great insight for his children. I remember my sisters and brother rushing in after playing kickball or riding bikes with neighborhood kids excited to share the adventures of our days around the dinner table. I remember lively conversation, and no matter how heated some of those conversations got, dinner was always a time to connect with each other as a family. Dinner is special to me. Dinner's simplicity brought our family, our relationships, and each other together back then, and today it is my family's cherished time to gather.

I bring many of those simple traditions to my own family when it comes to dinnertime. I may not be as formal as my dad and mom, but family time around the table with a home-cooked meal is still important to this day. As I prepare meals for my family and friends, it is short and simple, because we are rushing off to soccer practice, or the kids have friends coming over, or it's been a hectic week and we all need a special meal to help us reconnect. I often shout so everyone at home knows dinner is ready when it really isn't, so they can start meandering from wherever they are to the table. We always have room for more since often the boys say, "Hey Mom, do you have enough food for a friend(s) to eat with us?" They always know the answer: yes. I just like that they ask!

These recipes are about family. They are flexible and are designed to get your family around that dinner table for some quality time together. There are those simple and quick meals to make before or after a game, but also recipes to enjoy when the family has more time to gather around the dinner table and connect.

simple chicken

4 boneless skinless chicken breasts, fat removed

¼ cup olive oil

4 teaspoons minced garlic

1 teaspoon Italian seasoning

Salt and pepper, to taste

This is the basic of basics when it comes to cooking quick and tasty chicken. It is a time-tested, restaurant-like preparation that involves starting your chicken breasts in a sauté pan and finishing them in the oven.

Remember you can add or omit the garlic and seasonings as you see fit depending on what your chicken's final purpose is. For example, you could add rosemary to season if you were going to serve the chicken breasts with rosemary flavored potatoes. Or you could cut down on the Italian seasoning and add fajita seasonings if you were going to slice the chicken and add it to tacos. The idea here is that chicken breasts are like a blank canvas, and this recipe is just a jumping off point to peak your culinary creativity. Here is how it goes:

Place chicken on a cutting board, place plastic wrap over chicken, and tenderize with a meat mallet. With kitchen scissors remove any fat and discard. Place chicken breasts in a large bowl or dish and pour olive oil over them. Add minced garlic, Italian seasoning, and salt and pepper. Coat the chicken breasts with oil and seasonings. (Important: Always remember to wash your hands with hot soapy water before and after handling raw meat.)

Turn your oven to high broil and preheat. Position oven rack in the center. Since this is a restaurant type preparation, there may be a bit of smoke. Heat an oven-safe large sauté pan to high until it starts to smoke a bit. Now drizzle a bit of olive oil into the pan and immediately put chicken breast into the hot pan. Allow each chicken breast to brown (caramelized) on each side for about 3 minutes. Once both sides are browned, place the sauté pan into the oven on broil. Allow the chicken breasts to broil for about 5 minutes. They will plump up as they cook. Breasts should be firm when tested with your finger. Remove chicken from oven and pan, allowing them to table rest for about 5 minutes before serving.

Prep chicken this way ahead of time and put it in the fridge to use later for pastas, Mexican dishes, soups, salads, sandwiches, or a quick on-the-go dinner. Enjoy!

Serves 4

simple grilled steaks

ingredients

4 (12-ounce) ribeye or tri-tip steaks

Kosher salt

¼ cup olive oil

4 teaspoons minced garlic

1 teaspoon Italian seasoning

Pepper

Dash Worcestershire sauce

½ teaspoon cumin

½ teaspoon paprika

Lay the steaks out on a sheet pan and trim off the fat to your liking.

Sprinkle steaks with kosher salt, cover, and allow to sit for about 30 minutes. This gets the meat's juices following. Now drizzle olive oil on steaks and use your hands to coat each steak completely.

Add garlic, Italian seasoning, salt and pepper, dash of Worcestershire sauce, cumin, and paprika. Make sure the meat is covered on both sides with the seasoning.

Be sure to start with a clean grill. Heat your grill to high. Spray the heated grill with nonstick cooking spray, then add steaks with the tapered end of each steak facing toward you on the grill. After about 3 minutes, flip the steaks over so the tapered end is now facing away from you, and grill on this side for 3 minutes. Flip one last time so the tapered end is facing you. Grill for another 3 minutes and test with your finger for desired doneness. (The amount of grilling time depends on how thick each steak is and what your preference is for meat temperature.) Enjoy!

> " Who doesn't like steak? This tastes amazing when grilled correctly. It's a great backyard BBQ party with friends or just the family. A great Father's Day meal along with grilled hamburgers. The boys love the simplicity of steak, and Molly and I always split one. And of course we always need BBQ sauce for Jacob. Enjoy with roasted potatoes, a tossed green salad, and maybe finish the meal off with an ice cream sundae. Boneless steak is more versatile for fajitas, stir-fry, soups/stews. . .the possibilities are endless. "

Note:

The best type of fat in red meat is the internal fat. A nicely marbleized steak is judged by the light white strands of fat crossing through the fillet or cut. Marbled fat is contained in the meat itself, not around the outside.

Serves 4

simple salmon

ingredients

1 side of salmon, skinned and scaled

Olive oil

Salt and pepper

1 tablespoon minced garlic

2 limes, zested and juiced

½ cup white wine

¼ cup soy sauce

1 bunch green onions, sliced

With tweezers, remove the pin bones in your skinless side of salmon. With a sharp knife cut the side of salmon into fillets, about 4 inches long. In a medium dish, drizzle some olive oil to coat the fillet, then sprinkle with salt and pepper on both sides. Add garlic and coat the fillets again with more olive oil.

In a small bowl, add the juice of 2 limes, lime zest, white wine, soy sauce, and sliced green onion. Stir to combine and set aside.

Heat large sauté pan on high. Drizzle olive oil into the pan. Place salmon fillets into the hot pan. Allow the fillets to sauté on high for 3 to 4 minutes. Using tongs, flip each fillet and cook until both sides are caramelized. Make sure the cover for the sauté pan is handy, and add the white wine soy mixture to the hot pan. Be careful of the steam. Cover the sauté pan and reduce heat to medium. Steam for about 5 to 7 minutes to infuse the mixture into the fillets. Check the inside of the salmon to ensure it is cooked throughout. Try with wild rice or on a salad, or serve with quinoa, fresh veggies, tossed salad, and crusty bread. Enjoy!

Things to remember about salmon:

You may not want to use the skin on the bottom, pin bones on top, and the belly, that extra side part. If you don't mind the skin, then sauté or grill the salmon as is. To remove the belly, use long, smooth slicing motions; do not use the knife in a sawing motion. If you prefer no skin, use a cloth to hold the smallest end of the salmon so it doesn't slip out of your hand. Place a sharp knife, on an angle, very close to the edge of the skin and salmon, and slice in one long back and forth motion, separating the salmon fillet from the skin. Now you'll have a nice skinless fillet of salmon. If you don't want the bones and/or find pin bones, usually along the middle of the salmon, rub your finger down the center and you'll feel them. Use scissors or small pliers (used for food only) and gently pull each bone at an angle away from you. The bones should easily slide out; you shouldn't have to force them. Now the salmon is ready to prep as above.

Serves 4 to 6

amy's pork fried rice

ingredients

Olive oil

Salt and pepper

2 pork loin chops, boneless, tenderized,
   and cut into thin strips (or you can substitute with shrimp, as well)

½ teaspoon minced garlic

1 teaspoon freshly grated ginger

3 cups rice (brown is what I like best,
   but any white rice is fine)

1 carrot

3 green onions

½ cup frozen peas

2 eggs, beaten

1 tablespoon sesame seed oil

4 teaspoons low-sodium soy sauce
   (or adjust to your taste)

1 teaspoon sesame seeds, toasted

Cilantro, roughly chopped, for garnish

> *My family often enjoys going out for Chinese food, but I enjoy making something similar in my own kitchen. Home is where I'd rather eat most of our family dinners. Going out to eat was always a luxury growing up. Regardless, this is one of my versions of fried rice. My kids gobble this meal up. It's easy to adjust the quantity, and I'm always prepared for more people to join our kitchen table, which usually happens.*

Heat oil in a large sauté pan over medium heat. Salt and pepper pork loin strips and sauté for approximately 5 to 10 minutes, until no longer pink. Add garlic and ginger to the pan, heat for another minute. Remove from stove and set aside. Once cooled, remove pork loins and chop into bite-sized pieces; set aside. Meanwhile cook rice according to package directions, cool, and set aside.

Now, dice carrots and green onions. Heat a large sauté pan or wok to medium high. Drizzle with a little olive oil, add carrots, green onions, and peas and sauté for about 3 to 4 minutes. Add the diced pork to the vegetables, and sauté for 2 minutes. Heat a small sauté pan to medium. Spray pan with nonstick cooking spray, add eggs, and cook until they are almost an omelet. Remove egg from pan and dice into bite-sized pieces. Combine cooked rice, sesame oil, egg, and soy sauce in the large sauté pan or wok. Cook everything together until heated thoroughly, about 5 to 10 minutes. Top with toasted sesame seeds and cilantro. Enjoy!

Serves 6

meat &
red sauce pasta

ingredients

1 (1-pound) box spaghetti pasta

3 tablespoons olive oil, divided

3 teaspoons minced garlic

½ yellow onion, finely diced

½ pound mild Italian sausage

½ pound 94 percent lean ground beef

1 teaspoon Italian seasoning

½ cup red wine

1 (15-ounce) can diced tomatoes, drained

1 (15-ounce) can tomato sauce

Salt and pepper, to taste

1 cup shaved Parmesan cheese

Bring a large pot of water to boil, and add a dash of salt to it. Add pasta and stir often, cooking pasta until al dente, about 8 to 10 minutes. Drain pasta and wash with cold water, tossing with hands to clean it and cool it down. Strain excess water, turn pasta into a bowl, drizzle with 2 tablespoons olive oil and a dash of salt, toss with hands to coat, and set aside.

Heat a large saucepan to high. Add 1 tablespoon olive oil, and then add garlic and diced onion. Lower heat and sauté until garlic and onions become soft and translucent. Remove casing and break apart sausage into chunks. Return heat to high and crumble ground beef, sausage, and Italian seasoning into pan. Sauté for 5 minutes, using a wooden spoon to break the mixture up, until the meat browns. Deglaze pan with red wine and reduce heat to a simmer. Add diced tomatoes and tomato sauce. Stir to combined and bring back to a simmer. Add salt and pepper to taste. Cook sauce for another 5 minutes until flavors develop. Add ½ of the Parmesan cheese to the sauce and stir until it melts. Cheese may clump but just keep stirring it.

Add precooked spaghetti to the sauce. Using tongs or a pasta spoon, toss and coat your pasta with the meat sauce. Plate your pasta and garnish with a good amount of freshly shaved Parmesan cheese and serve with fresh warm bread. Enjoy!

My Zachary loves spaghetti and will request it at nearly every birthday. Every time Zach is hungry, and especially before soccer, it's his first request. Pasta is one of those versatile ingredients you can do anything with. In this version, it's all about sausage, ground beef, and a little red wine. This recipe is amazing as leftovers after the flavors really have a chance to show themselves. I normally make extra for that very reason.

Serves 6

> My kids have watched reruns of The Brady Bunch and whenever we have pork chops it reminds them of when Peter said, "Pork chops and apple sauce?" Pork is truly the other white meat. You can do a lot with it, and this is one of my kids' favorites. Pork chops and apples. My Molly doesn't like meat bone-in, so I often get boneless pork chops, or I just buy a bone-out cut. It is less expensive anyway.

roast pork WITH
spiced apples

ingredients

Pork:

2 teaspoons kosher salt

½ teaspoon freshly ground black pepper

4 cloves garlic

1 teaspoon paprika

1 teaspoon cinnamon

1 tablespoon freshly grated ginger

1 orange, zested

3 pork tenderloins (about 1½ pounds each)

3 tablespoons olive oil

Spiced apples:

1 tablespoon olive oil

1 teaspoon minced garlic

6 Pippin apples, peeled, quartered, and sliced

¾ cup dried cranberries

1 cup brown sugar

⅓ cup honey

⅓ cup apple juice

1 teaspoon cinnamon

½ teaspoon cumin

½ teaspoon coriander

¼ teaspoon pumpkin pie spice

¼ cup (½ stick) butter, cut into pats

For the pork:

Preheat the oven to 400°F. In a small bowl, combine salt, pepper, garlic, paprika, cinnamon, grated ginger, and orange zest. Drizzle pork loins with olive oil and rub it in. Rub seasoning mix onto each of the pork tenderloins. Set aside to cook later.

For the spiced apples:

In a medium saucepan, heat olive oil, add garlic, and sauté on medium for about a minute. Be sure not to brown the garlic. Add apple slices and cranberries and sauté for a minute. Add brown sugar, honey, apple juice, cinnamon, cumin, coriander, and pumpkin pie spice. Stir constantly to combine. Raise heat to dissolve the sugars, boil for a moment, then turn down and simmer. Allow syrup to thicken on low heat for about 10 minutes. When the sauce thickens, remove from heat and whisk in one pat of butter at a time. Set aside.

In a large ovenproof skillet, heat a few tablespoons of olive oil over high heat. Add pork and sear on all sides, 2 minutes per side, until caramelized and brown. Place skillet with pork loin in preheated oven and roast for 8 to 10 minutes. Remove from the oven and let rest for 5 minutes before cutting. Slicing on the bias, cut each tenderloin into 4 or 5 pieces. Plate pork loin and pour spoonfuls of the spiced apples over the pork loin medallions. Serve with any rice dish, potatoes, or green salad. Enjoy!

Serves 6 to 8

any night stir-fry

1 pound boneless, skinless chicken breast
(or tenders, cut into pieces)

6 tablespoons sesame oil, divided

2 teaspoons cornstarch

2 teaspoons minced garlic

2 green onions

2 teaspoons peeled and shaved fresh ginger

2 tablespoons light brown sugar, packed

2 tablespoons soy sauce

Salt and pepper

¾ cup canned low-sodium chicken broth

1 tablespoon cornstarch

2 teaspoons minced garlic

2 teaspoons minced fresh ginger

1 cup sliced baby carrots

3 green onions, cut on the bias

1 red bell pepper, cut into slices

1 cup broccoli florets

1 tablespoon hoisin sauce

3 tablespoons soy sauce

1 tablespoon sambal sauce (or chili flakes)

4 servings jasmine rice, steamed in rice
cooker, prepared just before starting stir-fry
(If you do not have a steamer, cook
according to package directions.)

Place raw chicken pieces in a large bowl. Add sesame oil, cornstarch, garlic, green onions, shaved ginger, brown sugar, soy sauce, salt, and pepper. Combine ingredients to coat chicken. Set aside for about 10 minutes to absorb flavor.

In a medium microwave-proof bowl heat chicken broth to lukewarm. Remove and mix in cornstarch, dissolving it to making a slurry; set aside for later.

Heat a large sauté pan over high heat. Add 2 tablespoons sesame oil to pan. Add garlic, ginger, baby carrots, and green onions. Sauté for 1 minute, then add bell pepper and broccoli florets. Sauté for 2 minutes so veggies are crisp and cooked but not losing their color. Remove veggies and set aside.

Heat another large sauté pan on high, then add 2 tablespoons sesame oil. Add chicken pieces and sauté, and allow to brown for 4 minutes. Add hoisin, soy, and sambal sauces to the pan. Toss chicken to coat. Add cooked veggies to the pan, then toss with chicken to cook for about a minute. Add chicken broth/cornstarch mixture and toss chicken and veggies to coat. Allow sauce to cook with the stir-fry and thicken, bringing it to a boil. Add salt and pepper to taste as desired. Reduce heat. Plate a cup of rice for each serving, then spoon stir-fry over rice. Garnish with toasted sesame seeds, green onions, and cilantro leaves. Enjoy!

Serves 4

> " *This recipe is good, quick, and I like making it often. When we have a lot going on at home it's a good dinner to put together to gather everyone around the dinner table, at least for a few minutes. Jacob loves chicken, and I continue to try and get him to eat more veggies with this recipe. I have sometimes substituted beef for chicken and beef broth for chicken broth. For convenience you can get some of the veggies already precut, but I like fresh!* "

hearty beef stew

ingredients

2 pounds beef stew meat, or leftover beef
    roast, cut into bite-sized pieces
1 cup flour
Salt and pepper
⅓ cup olive oil
1 large sweet yellow onion
6 ounces tomato paste
1 cup red wine
2 cups beef broth
1 bay leaf

1 large (14.5 ounces) can diced tomatoes
8 ounces baby carrots
1 teaspoon thyme
1 teaspoon rosemary
1 teaspoon minced garlic
1 pound Yukon gold potatoes
1 cup frozen peas, optional
¼ cup roughly chopped fresh
    flat-leaf parsley

In a medium bowl add cubed beef and toss with flour, salt, and pepper.

Drizzle 2 to 3 tablespoons olive oil in a large stockpot and brown meat in batches, careful not to overcrowd the pan. Remove to a roasting pan or baking dish. Chop onions and reheat stockpot on high. Add onions and sauté until opaque, 5 to 7 minutes. Add tomato paste, wine, beef broth, bay leaf, diced tomatoes, carrots, thyme, rosemary, and garlic.

Cover and simmer for one hour, remembering to stir often. Meanwhile, cut up potatoes into ½-inch chunks. Heat a large sauté pan on high and drizzle with 2 tablespoons olive oil. Add potatoes and sauté until tender, not soft. Add potatoes, peas (if using), and the cooked cubed beef to the stockpot with the veggies. Simmer for another 20 minutes. Add parsley. Serve in large bowls with crusty bread. Enjoy!

Serves 6 to 8

chicken enchiladas

ingredients

Sauce:

4 tablespoons vegetable oil

4 tablespoons butter

2 tablespoons minced garlic

2 tablespoons flour

½ cup chili powder

4 cups low-sodium chicken stock

2 (10-ounce) cans tomato paste

2 teaspoons dried oregano

2 teaspoons ground cumin

2 limes, juiced

A few dashes of hot sauce to give it a little zing

¼ cup cilantro, not chopped, stems removed

1 teaspoon salt

Enchiladas:

2 cups rice (or omit and serve Mexican style
   rice on the side)

2 tablespoons olive oil

2 teaspoons minced garlic

¼ cup diced green onions

2 pounds precooked chicken breast,
   shredded or diced (see Simple Chicken
   recipe, *pg. 52*)

2 teaspoons cumin powder

2 chipotle chilies, seeded and diced (or ¼
   teaspoon chipotle seasoning)

1 lime, zested and juiced

½ teaspoon chili powder

Salt and pepper

1 (15-ounce) can black beans

1 small can (6 ounces) black olives, roughly
   chopped

2 cups shredded Cheddar cheese

2 cups shredded jack cheese

About 16 corn or flour tortillas

Dollop of sour cream

¼ cup roughly chopped cilantro

¼ cup sliced green onion, for garnish

For the sauce:

In a medium saucepan, heat oil and butter, then add garlic and sauté quickly. Add flour, stirring with a wooden spoon to break up clumps, and cook flour until it resembles a paste. Cook for an additional minute. Add chili powder and cook for 30 seconds. Whisk in chicken stock, tomato paste, oregano, cumin, lime juice, hot sauce, and whole cilantro leaves.

Bring sauce to a boil, then reduce heat and simmer for 12 minutes. The sauce will thicken. Add salt to taste. Remove from heat and pour into a blender. Puree in blender for about 1 minute then return to pot and set aside.

chicken enchiladas

> " *I have been making these enchiladas for years. My methods have changed a little, but I often make them after Thanksgiving using leftover turkey. It's something different from ground beef or chicken. That's the fun of making enchiladas—you can use chicken, beef, or turkey. My family loves them. They wait all day, never leaving the house, and even invite friends over when they know I am making enchiladas. I always know I need to make extra. They're homemade, fresh, and just good. I don't make them often, but when the family asks, I can't say no. These enchiladas do not last long. They may take a little time to prepare, but they are well worth it. FYI—they are even better as leftovers.* "

For the enchiladas:

Cook rice according to directions. Heat a large sauté pan over medium to high heat, then add olive oil, garlic, and diced green onions, and sauté for a minute. Add chicken, cumin, chilies, lime zest, lime juice, chili powder, and salt and pepper. You can add a splash of enchilada sauce as well if desired. Sauté for one or two minutes, and then add the amount of black beans, black olives, and rice you prefer. Set aside for later to fill tortillas and assemble enchiladas. Place cheeses into separate bowls.

Preheat oven to 350°F. Reheat the enchilada sauce until it is warm. Microwave corn tortillas for 30 seconds to a minute to make them pliable. Coat the bottom of a 9 by 13-inch baking dish with cooking spray. Add a ladleful of enchilada sauce, and sprinkle the bottom with both cheeses. Add about a ¼ cup of the chicken filling to the center of tortilla, and sprinkle with cheeses. Roll up tortilla, covering the filling with edges, and arranging each lengthwise in pan seam-side down. Repeat until all 16 tortillas are filled. Pour the remaining sauce over enchiladas, ensuring all tortillas are covered. Top with remaining cheeses and put in oven for 15 minutes until heated thoroughly with the cheese melting and sauce bubbling. Remove from oven and cool for 10 minutes. Garnish the top of each enchilada with a dollop of sour cream, chopped cilantro, and green onions. Serve with Mexican style rice and refried or black beans. Enjoy!

Serves 8

tilapia WITH homemade pesto & quinoa

ingredients

4 tilapia fillets
1 tablespoon olive oil
½ lime, juiced
1 tablespoon minced garlic
½ cup pesto, store-bought or homemade
 (see below)

For quinoa:
2 tablespoons olive oil
½ small yellow onion, finely chopped
½ tablespoon minced garlic
1 cup quinoa, uncooked

2 cups canned chicken stock
1 Roma tomato, roughly chopped
3 stems fresh basil, roughly chopped

For homemade pesto:
⅓ cup pine nuts
1 tablespoon minced garlic
2 cups fresh basil
½ cup olive oil
½ cup grated Parmesan cheese
½ teaspoon each, salt and pepper

In a shallow dish add tilapia fillets, 1 tablespoon olive oil, lime juice, garlic, and salt and pepper. Coat gently with hands.

For quinoa:
In a medium saucepan add olive oil and chopped onion. Sauté on low for 3 minutes until opaque. Add garlic and sauté another minute. Add quinoa and brown for 2 minutes, then add chicken stock, bring to a boil, and reduce to a simmer. Cover for 10 minutes or until tender. Remove from heat and set aside.

For homemade pesto:
Toast pine nuts over low in a small sauté pan until light brown. In a food processor pulse the pine nuts until fine. Add garlic and basil leaves and pulse until pureed. Now stream in olive oil while running the food processor. Scrape sides and add Parmesan cheese, salt, and pepper. Pulse again to combine and check seasoning.

Heat a large sauté pan to high, add 1 tablespoon olive oil, and add tilapia fillets. Sauté on high, browning for 2 minutes on each side. Once cooked, remove fillets from heat and leave in pan.
Stir tomato and basil into quinoa, then add a pinch of salt and pepper to taste. Plate quinoa, place tilapia fillet on top, and spread 2 teaspoons of pesto on top of the tilapia. Enjoy!

Serves 4

winter chili

4 tablespoons olive oil, divided

½ pound beef round, fat trimmed and cut into bite-sized pieces

1 tablespoon flour

1 pound 94 percent lean ground beef

2 medium yellow onions, chopped

1 cup corn kernels, canned or frozen

1 green bell pepper, seeded and diced

4 teaspoons minced garlic

1 jalapeño pepper, seeded and diced

2 tablespoons ground cumin

2 tablespoons chili powder

1 teaspoon paprika

1 teaspoon dried oregano

1 teaspoon Italian seasoning

½ teaspoon nutmeg

½ cup beef stock

½ cup apple juice

2 (14-ounce) cans diced tomatoes

1 bay leaf

3 cans (14.5 ounces) black or pinto beans, drained

Salt and pepper, to taste

¼ cup chopped fresh cilantro

½ cup shredded Cheddar cheese, optional

Heat a large Dutch oven or saucepan over medium to high heat, then add 2 tablespoons of olive oil. In a large bowl, season beef round with salt and pepper and toss with flour to coat. Add beef to saucepan and brown on all sides, cooking over medium heat for 3 minutes. Add ground beef and brown as well. Remove meat onto a plate, leaving the oil in the pan.

Add 2 more tablespoons of olive oil to the pan and then add onions, corn, and bell pepper. Sauté over medium until golden brown and translucent, about 5 minutes. Add garlic, jalapeño, cumin, chili powder, paprika, oregano, Italian seasoning, and nutmeg, stirring to combine seasonings.

Add beef stock and apple juice to the pan. Bring to a simmer, scraping the pan. Simmer for 5 minutes. Add diced tomatoes with juice, a bay leaf, and the meat. Stir to combine all ingredients and return to a simmer, cover, and cook on low for about 2 hours, stirring occasionally.

After chili base reduces, add the drained beans, stir to combine, return back to a simmer, cover, and cook over low heat for another 30 minutes. Remove bay leaf. Add salt and pepper to taste. Add fresh cilantro and Cheddar cheese (if using). Serve with cornbread or sour dough bread. Enjoy!

Serves 6 to 8

roast WITH country veggies & potatoes

ingredients

4 tablespoons unsalted butter,
   room temperature
2 garlic cloves, pressed
1 teaspoon chopped fresh rosemary
¾ teaspoon coarse kosher salt
½ teaspoon freshly cracked black pepper
1 (3-pound) boneless beef loin New York
   strip roast (or eye of round roast)
3 medium potatoes, peeled, and cut into
   2 x ½ x ½-inch strips
4 medium carrots, peeled, quartered
   lengthwise, and cut crosswise into
   1½ - to 2-inch pieces

4 celery ribs, peeled and cut into
   2 x ½ x ½-inch strips
1 large yellow onion, peeled and cut
   crosswise into ¼-inch-thick slices
1 pound butternut squash
6 tablespoons olive oil
½ tablespoon chopped fresh rosemary
   (or 1 tablespoon dried)
½ tablespoon fresh thyme (or
   1 tablespoon dried)
½ tablespoon fresh oregano
   (or 1 tablespoon dried)
Coarse kosher salt and pepper, to taste

Cream together room temperature butter, garlic, 1 teaspoon rosemary, salt, and pepper in a small bowl. Place beef, fat-side up, in 9 by 13 by 2-inch roasting pan, and, with your hands, spread butter paste over roast.

Preheat oven to 450°F. Place veggies in a large bowl or roasting pan. Drizzle on olive oil, add rosemary, thyme, oregano, and salt and pepper. Toss to coat the veggies. Spread veggies in roasting pan and roast in oven for 20 to 25 minutes until veggies are slightly tender. Remove veggies from oven. Place roast on top and return to oven to roast for 15 minutes at 450°F, then reduce heat to 350°F. Roast another 30 to 40 minutes, basting occasionally with pan juices, or until meat gets to about 130 to 140 degrees, or medium rare to medium, and continue until the veggies are brown. Remove from oven and allow to rest for 10 minutes before serving. Enjoy!

I love Sunday dinners. After a long hectic week, I love having the time to make a fabulous beef roast. The family comes together, and we update each other on what we've been up to, tell stories, and enjoy each other. I know it sounds shocking, but the kids actually sit at the dinner table to hang out and take a breather!

Serves 6

mini meatloaf dinner

2 tablespoons olive oil

½ medium onion, finely diced

2 teaspoons minced garlic

1½ pounds 94 percent lean ground beef

2 tablespoons Dijon mustard

¼ cup tomato paste

¾ cup bread crumbs

½ cup grated Parmesan cheese

2 eggs

1 teaspoon Worcestershire sauce

1 teaspoon balsamic vinegar

2 tablespoons Italian seasoning

1 teaspoon salt

½ teaspoon cracked black pepper

Meatloaf Glaze:

½ cup ketchup

1 teaspoon ground cumin

Dash Worcestershire sauce

1 tablespoon honey

Preheat oven to 375°F. Heat a small sauté pan with olive oil. Add diced onion and minced garlic. Sauté over low heat until onions are translucent. Remove and cool for 5 to 10 minutes.

In a large bowl combine ground beef, Dijon mustard, tomato paste, bread crumbs, and Parmesan cheese. Mix with your hands until all ingredients are combined. In a small bowl, whip eggs lightly with Worcestershire sauce and balsamic vinegar. Add mixture to ground beef with Italian seasoning, salt, and pepper, mixing to combine.

For the glaze, combine all ingredients in a small bowl and whisk; set aside.

Form 8 to 9 oval shape meatloaves and place on prepared baking sheet. Place a spoonful of glaze on each mini meatloaf. Bake in oven for 25 to 30 minutes until each mini meatloaf is completely cooked. Serve with potatoes of any kind and fresh steamed and buttered veggies. Enjoy!

Serves 6

> " *I grew up eating meatloaf as a kid. I don't know why, but this was many families' Monday, midweek, or Sunday dinner. You could always count on it. Everyone loves Mom's meatloaf. Now that I'm a mom cooking for my four kids, this has become a staple for our family meals, as well. I like making mini meatloaves instead of one loaf because you can make each one to size, and it makes a wonderful meatloaf sandwich the next day. I've added Dijon mustard for a little zing. The meatloaf comes out tender and richer in flavor. My kids always come to the dinner table hungry, and at the end often ask if they can have another mini meatloaf.* "

pasta carbonara
WITH PEAS

ingredients

1 cup French bread crumbs

½ cup chopped roasted walnuts

1 pound linguine (or spaghetti)

2 tablespoons olive oil

6 to 8 slices bacon

1 teaspoon minced garlic

2 teaspoons lemon zest

1 cup frozen peas

2 eggs

¼ cup half and half (or cream if not worried about fat)

½ cup shredded Parmesan cheese

2 tablespoons fresh flat-leaf parsley

Salt and pepper

Start with enough stale French bread to make one cup of bread crumbs—worst case scenario, use store-bought bread crumbs. In a medium sauté pan, or in the oven, toast walnuts until browned.

In a large pot, boil water and cook pasta as directed. Once al dente, drain, wash, and return to pot, drizzle with a little olive oil and a dash of salt, toss, and set aside.

In a medium sauté pan, cook bacon until crisp. Remove and drain on paper towels. Once cool, crumble bacon into a dish and set aside. In large saucepan, combine pasta, bacon, garlic, lemon zest, and peas, and heat over medium. Now whisk eggs and half and half into the pasta mixture. Keep on medium and toss to combine, then add Parmesan cheese. Toss again on medium until pasta is completely coated and sauce is combined. Place in large serving bowl and top with toasted bread crumbs, walnuts, and parsley. Enjoy!

Serves 4 to 6

roast new york strip loin WITH GARLIC-HERB CRUST

1 (5-pound) boneless beef loin New York strip roast, fat trimmed to ¼ inch

4 garlic cloves

8 fresh sage leaves

4 teaspoons fresh thyme leaves

4 teaspoons fresh rosemary

4 teaspoons olive oil

4 teaspoons salt

1½ teaspoons fresh cracked black pepper

Salt the meat and let rest for 30 minutes.

Start food processor and drop garlic cloves in; pulse until finely chopped. Add sage, thyme, rosemary, oil, salt and pepper, and pulse until a paste forms. Pat meat dry with paper towels. Rub meat completely with herb paste. Cover and chill at least 3 hours. (Can be made 1 day ahead.)

Preheat oven to 450°F. Place meat, fat-side up, on rack in roasting pan. Roast meat 15 minutes. Reduce oven temperature to 350°F. Roast until meat thermometer registers 130°F for medium-rare, or 140°F for medium, about 35 to 40 minutes. Remove from oven. Let stand 20 minutes. Cut cross-wise into ⅓-inch-thick slices. Arrange slices on platter. Enjoy!

Serves 10

" *New York strip loin, also called top loin of beef, is a succulent, elegant roast. If you want a lot of leftovers (they are great for sandwiches), use a seven-pound roast and multiply the seasonings by 1½. Either way, have your butcher trim some of the fat, leaving about ¼ inch for the best flavor. As an entrée, uncork a cabernet sauvignon or Oregon pinot noir. Serve with your favorite side dish and hearty crusty bread. This works great with most beef roast, such as eye of round. It has great flavor, too. I'll make a roast anytime, but sometimes I'll save it for a Sunday when I want the family to eat together and just catch up on life over a fantastic dinner!* "

mike d.'s hamburger pie

ingredients

5 or 6, medium, russet potatoes

1 pound 94 percent lean ground beef

Salt and pepper, to taste

Olive oil

½ onion, finely chopped

1 teaspoon minced garlic

1 teaspoon Italian seasoning

1 teaspoon fresh parsley

Dash cayenne pepper, for an extra kick

1 (14.5-ounce) can tomato sauce

½ cup light cream

1 can (14.5 ounces) green beans, drained

¼ cup butter

½ cup light sour cream (amount depends on desired consistency)

¾ cup Cheddar cheese

Dash paprika

Preheat oven to 350°F. Peel and quarter potatoes, then place in large pot of cold water and bring to a boil. Boil potatoes as you would when making mashed potatoes, until a knife goes through cleanly. Drain potatoes and set aside.

In a medium sauté pan cook ground beef, seasoning with salt and pepper. After meat is cooked, remove from heat, and drain fat. Drizzle olive oil in a small pan and sauté onions and garlic until translucent. Add to meat. Add Italian seasoning, parsley, dash of cayenne, tomato sauce, light cream, and green beans. Cook until heated and combined.

Now mash potatoes, adding butter and light sour cream until smooth with a stiff consistency. In a 9 by 13-inch baking dish, layer spoonfuls of meat mixture to cover bottom of pan, then layer potato mixture on top of meat. Continue alternating layers of meat and potatoes, finishing with potato mixture. Sprinkle Cheddar cheese on top of potatoes, adding a dash of paprika. Place in oven and bake for 30 minutes until heated through. You may want to put foil over the top for the first 25 minutes, then remove to brown the cheese, depending on your oven.

Goes great with a green salad and dinner rolls. Enjoy!

Serves 6

> " *This is the American version of shepherd's pie. I've made this many times even before knowing our good friend Mike D. He always liked some kick to comfort food, hence the cayenne pepper. He passed this recipe onto my kids and me. I've added more spices to expand the flavor, but this is Mike, tried and true. When Zach was in speech class and needed a recipe for a demonstration, I knew he would make this special recipe. Obviously it's a guy thing—meat and potatoes. I make this dish often because it reminds us of Mike, a great friend. It helps us remember how much he is a part of our family. Memories, sharing, and welcoming others to your table is what life is about!* "

fish tacos
WITH PEACH CILANTRO SALSA

Tacos:
6 to 8 tilapia fillets
½ teaspoon cumin
½ teaspoon paprika
½ lime, juiced
Dash cayenne pepper
Dash salt and ground pepper
1 tablespoon olive oil
1 fresh corncob roasted (or good quality
 canned corn)
½ cup black beans
¼ bunch cilantro, roughly chopped
8 to 10 corn tortillas
Shredded lettuce

4 green onions, sliced
2 Roma tomatoes, chopped
Shredded jack or Cheddar cheese, optional

Peach Cilantro Salsa:
1 cup chopped fresh peaches, skins
 removed
¼ cup chopped red onion
2 cloves garlic, minced
1½ teaspoons minced fresh ginger
1 teaspoon chipotle seasoning
⅓ cup chopped cilantro
½ lime, juiced
Salt and pepper

Prepare Peach Cilantro Salsa ahead of time. In a small bowl, add peaches, red onion, garlic, fresh ginger, chipotle seasoning, cilantro, lime juice, and salt and pepper. Mix thoroughly to combine. Cover and refrigerate until tacos are prepared.

In a shallow dish, lay out fish fillets then add cumin, paprika, lime juice, cayenne pepper, salt and pepper. With your hands rub spices into the fish to coat. Heat a large sauté pan on high, add olive oil, and sauté fish until done, about 3 to 4 minutes per side.

Break up fish into a medium bowl. Roast corn with a little olive oil, then slice corn off of cob. If using canned corn, place corn on baking sheet in a 425°F oven, and roast for 10 to 15 minutes. Remove and set aside. Heat up black beans in a small pan with a dash of salt and cilantro.

Heat up tortillas in microwave with a sprinkle of water for about a minute. Fill corn tortillas with fish, roasted corn, black beans, shredded lettuce, green onion, and top with peach salsa, chopped Roma tomatoes, and cheese (if using). Serve with fresh vegetables or roasted/grilled zucchini. Enjoy!

Serves 8 to 10

sweet endings

I think of cooking like bookends to the day. And if you have ever had a meal with me, you know I have to have dessert or something sweet to end the day. I like getting off to a great start with a solid breakfast. Then what carries me through the day is something fulfilling like Lite Lunch Fare to know I'll be able to get more done with the right fuel in my gas tank. But the day's not over with my kids' activities or a dinner that says there is still Time to Gather and break bread as a family. When my day is over, I have to end it with something sweet from Sweet Endings.

There is something about Sweet Endings that says I was really thinking of you and took some time to let you know it. So when my kids have been working hard at school or are tired after sports, or if Matt has been working on the farm or in all-day meetings, there's nothing like a Berry Peach Cobbler, a slice of Chocolate Potato Cake, or Amy's Everything Cookies that says you deserve this. Sweet Endings are recipes that, for years, have bookended my days and helped me show those I love just how much they mean to me.

potato chocolate cake

ingredients

1 to 2 small russet potatoes

1 cup lukewarm water

2 cups flour

¾ cup unsweetened Dutch cocoa powder

2¼ teaspoons baking powder

½ teaspoon baking soda

Pinch of salt

⅔ cup unsalted butter

2 cups granulated sugar

1 teaspoon pure vanilla extract

4 large eggs

Optional Additions:

3 teaspoons instant coffee crystals

1 cup miniature chocolate chips

½ cup toasted walnuts

> *This recipe was given to me by my good friend Mike. He told me his mom had often made this cake for him, especially for his birthday. Since I love to bake, I felt honored he would pass the recipe on to me. It was Mike's favorite chocolate cake recipe, and I would make it for him every year on his birthday. It's not too sweet, but has lots of chocolate flavor. All of my kids love this cake, especially Zach. You can add frosting or not; it's up to you. It's good either way. I sometimes drizzle melted semisweet chocolate chips on top and dust the cake with powdered sugar. It's an easy cake to dress up for special occasions, and it always reminds us of our friend Mike Detjen.*

Preheat oven to 350°F. Grease a 9 by 13-inch baking pan or regular size bundt pan, then dust lightly with flour or sugar. (I prefer a bundt pan.) Peel and quarter potatoes, then place in a large pot of cold water and bring to boil. Boil potatoes until a knife goes through cleanly. Drain the potatoes but do not add salt, butter, or milk.

In a small bowl, whisk in lukewarm water with the mashed potatoes. Do not overbeat. In a large bowl, sift together flour, cocoa powder, baking powder, baking soda, and a pinch of salt. (Optional: stir in chocolate chips and instant coffee.) Use an electric mixer with the paddle attachment to blend butter, sugar, and vanilla until fluffy. Add two eggs, one at a time, then beat at low speed until blended. Scrape the sides of the bowl and add the other two eggs. Beat at medium speed until completely combined and fluffy.

At low speed, add sifted dry ingredients in 3 additions, and add mashed potato mixture in 2 additions, ending with dry ingredients. Beat after each addition until blended. (Optional: stir in toasted walnuts.)

Pour batter in prepared pan and spread so that it is even all around pan. Bake in preheated oven for about 30 minutes until a toothpick comes out clean. Dust with powdered sugar or drizzle with melted chocolate. Enjoy!

Serves 8 to 10

bananas foster

ingredients

4 ripe, firm bananas, sliced

4 tablespoons unsalted butter

1 cup light brown sugar, packed

¾ teaspoon ground cinnamon

¼ cup banana liqueur

½ cup dark rum

1 pint vanilla ice cream

Melt the butter in a large skillet over medium heat. Add brown sugar and cinnamon, stirring, until the sugar dissolves, about 2 minutes. Add bananas to sauce, cook until bananas start to soften and brown, about 3 minutes.

Add banana liqueur, stirring to blend into sauce. Carefully add the rum and shake the pan back and forth to warm the rum and flame the pan. (Or, off the heat, carefully ignite the pan with a match and return to the heat.) Shake the pan back and forth, basting the bananas, until the flame dies.

Divide ice cream among four serving bowls. Using a large spoon, pour bananas over the ice cream. Serve immediately. Enjoy!

Serves 4

> *When the kids and I took a vacation to visit New Orleans and went to Brennan's Restaurant, the birthplace of Bananas Foster, I fell in love with this dessert. This is what I came up with to re-create that wonderful, delicious dessert I had with my family tableside. The booze cooks out, so don't worry, kiddos.*

pound cake WITH berries & ice cream

ingredients

Pound cake:

Nonstick cooking spray

1 tablespoon granulated sugar

2¼ cups flour

½ teaspoon baking soda

¼ teaspoon salt

¾ cup butter, room temperature

2 cups granulated sugar

1 teaspoon lemon extract

2 large eggs

1½ teaspoons grated lemon zest

8 ounces low-fat sour cream

2 tablespoons lemon juice

1 cup powdered sugar

Vanilla ice cream

Berries:

2 cups crushed frozen berries

¼ cup sugar

½ teaspoon vanilla

For the pound cake:

Preheat oven to 350°F. Coat bundt pan with cooking spray and dust with sugar, rotating to coat the pan. In a medium mixing bowl, combine flour, baking soda, and salt, and mix together. In a large mixing bowl, beat butter until light and fluffy. Gradually add sugar and lemon extract while beating. Add eggs one at a time, beating well after each egg; add lemon zest. Beat well until combined and light. Next, add flour mixture to butter mixture alternately with sour cream, beating at low speed.

Spoon batter into prepared bundt pan. Bake for 1 hour and 10 minutes until an inserted knife comes out clean. Cool in pan for 10 to 15 minutes. Remove from pan and cool completely. Combine 2 tablespoons lemon juice with powdered sugar, then drizzle glaze over top of cake.

For the berries:

Crush berries, then mix with sugar and vanilla. Set aside to set up for about 30 to 45 minutes. Pour over pound cake and top with ice cream. Enjoy!

Serves 10 to 12

any occasion cupcakes

1 box plain cake mix, chocolate, yellow, white
(or your kids' favorite)

1 vanilla instant pudding mix (or chocolate,
if chocolate cake mix)

¼ cup water

1 cup sour cream

1 cup vegetable oil

4 large eggs

1 teaspoon pure vanilla extract

2 (12-ounce) tubs of your preferred
premade icing

Various sprinkles (or other cake decorations)

> *These cupcakes are eaten up in no time! When I made cupcakes for my kids when they were in school they were a hit at parties or any time they had friends over. Mini cupcakes are a hit, too. This recipe is rich and reminds me of a pound cake. Wonderful. Why not have a kids cupcake decorating party — just saying!*

Preheat oven to 350°F, or as the box of cake mix directs. Be sure to put your rack in the center of the oven. Put 24 cupcake cups liners into 2 cupcake pans and set aside.

In an electric mixer bowl, add cake mix, instant pudding, water, sour cream, oil, eggs, and vanilla extract. Beat on low to combine then turn up to high speed to beat air into batter. Stop at least once to scrape the sides of the bowl. Once all the ingredients are combined scoop about ¼ cup of cake batter into each lined cupcake cup.

Bake cupcakes for 16 to 20 minutes, then test for doneness by pressing finger to their tops. They should spring back. Or check by inserting a toothpick or knife. If done, it will come out clean. Remove from oven and cool for 10 minutes. Remove cupcakes from pan and cool an additional 40 minutes.

Generously spread icing on the tops of the cupcakes. Depending on our kids, and their sugar intake, decorate with sprinkles, candies, or your favorite confectionary decorations. Enjoy!

Makes 24 cupcakes

pumpkin bread

ingredients

1 cup plus 4 tablespoons sour cream

4 teaspoons baking soda

2 teaspoons baking powder

2 cups butter, room temperature

4 cups granulated sugar

2 (14.5-ounce) cans pumpkin puree

1 tablespoon pumpkin pie spice

1 teaspoon cinnamon

½ teaspoon nutmeg

½ teaspoon ground ginger

4 eggs

½ cup vegetable oil

¼ teaspoon pure vanilla extract

8 cups all–purpose flour

2 teaspoons baking powder

1 teaspoon salt

Toasted chopped walnuts, optional

Halve the recipe if you do not want to make this much pumpkin bread. Then again, it's always nice to give a loaf away to that special friend or neighbor and let them know you're thinking of them.

Preheat your oven to 350°F. In a large mixing bowl, combine sour cream and baking soda; set aside. With a mixer, cream butter and sugar together until fluffy. Add sour cream mixture to the creamed butter on medium speed, mixing completely. In a small mixing bowl, combine pumpkin puree cinnamon, nutmeg, and ginger; whisk to combine. To pumpkin mixture, whisk in eggs one at a time, then add oil and vanilla. The batter should look a bit watery. Now add pumpkin mixture to the creamed butter mixture until well blended.

Sift flour, baking soda, baking powder, and salt into the pumpkin sugar mixture. Start mixer on low and then increase as flour is incorporated.

Spray loaf pans with cooking spray and pour about ¼ cup of sugar into each pan. Rotate until the sides of pans are covered. Pour batter into loaf pans and top with toasted walnuts (if using). Bake for 35 to 45 minutes until golden brown or inserted knife comes out clean. Cool on racks for 45 minutes. Serve immediately or wrap with plastic wrap and store in the freezer. Enjoy!

Makes approximately 2 to 3 loaves, depending on pan size

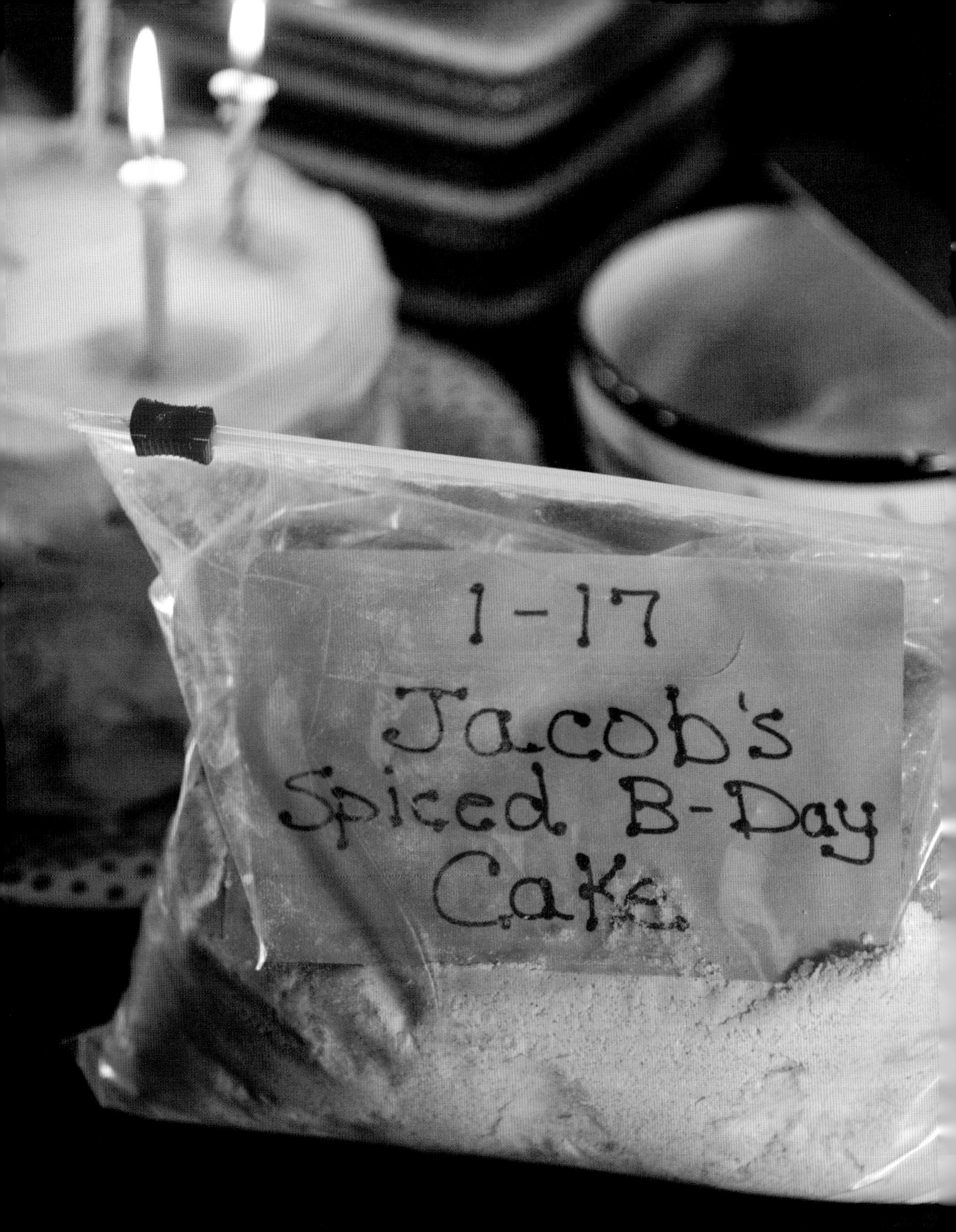
1-17
Jacob's
Spiced B-Day
Cake

birthday cake in a bag

ingredients

Dry ingredients:

2¼ cups cake flour

1 cup granulated sugar

2 teaspoons baking powder

1 teaspoon salt

½ teaspoon baking soda

2 tablespoons pumpkin pie spice

1 teaspoon cinnamon

Wet ingredients:

½ cup butter, room temperature

1 cup brown sugar, packed

3 eggs

1 teaspoon pure vanilla extract

1 cup light half and half

In a large bowl, sift together cake flour, sugar, baking powder, salt, baking soda, pumpkin pie spice, and cinnamon. Put all dry ingredients into a large resealable plastic bag. In a smaller resealable plastic bag, measure out your packed brown sugar, press to remove air, and seal the bag. Put this bag into the larger resealable plastic bag with dry ingredients. On one side of a 3 by 5-inch card write the type of cake you have prepped—Jacob's B-Day Spice Cake. And just in case, I always write the order in which the rest of the ingredients are added, the baking temp, and time.

> " Take any homemade cake recipe, measure the dry ingredients into a resealable plastic bag, write out the recipes on a card, have the wet ingredients on hand, and when the occasion calls, preheat that oven and break out your birthday cake in a bag! "

When a cake is needed . . . Preheat oven to 350°F. Grease and flour two 9-inch cake rounds.

Using an electric mixer, cream the softened butter with brown sugar until light and fluffy. Add one egg at a time until fluffy. Add vanilla, mixing on medium speed. Add the butter sugar mixture to dry ingredients, and then add half and half. Beat until fluffy. Add batter to pans and spread evenly. Bake 25 to 30 minutes at 350°F or until a toothpick comes out clean from center. Cool on rack and frost with your favorite frosting. For Jacob, I normally do cream cheese frosting with sprinkles.

Remember this can be done for any basic cake, brownie, or cookie recipe. Remember to store your bags in a cool dry place. After 6 months replace them, because the active ingredients will go bad. Enjoy!

Serves 8 to 10

strawberry rhubarb crisp

4 cups peeled and diced fresh rhubarb

4 cups prepped and halved fresh
  strawberries

½ cup granulated sugar

1½ teaspoons grated orange zest

1 tablespoon cornstarch

½ cup orange juice

Topping:

1 cup all-purpose flour

¼ cup granulated sugar

½ cup light brown sugar

½ teaspoon salt

1 cup quick-cooking oats

12 tablespoons (1½ sticks) butter, cold, diced

Ice cream or whipping cream, for serving

Preheat the oven to 350°F. Spray an 8 by 11-inch baking dish with cooking spray.

Toss rhubarb, strawberries, ½ cup granulated sugar, and orange zest together in a large bowl. In a measuring cup, dissolve cornstarch in orange juice, and then mix it into the rhubarb and strawberries. Toss to combine and pour into prepared baking dish.

For topping:

In a medium bowl combine flour, ¼ cup granulated sugar, brown sugar, salt, and oats. Once combined, cut in butter and mix until the dry ingredients are moist and resemble crumbs. Sprinkle the topping over the fruit, covering it completely. Put in oven and bake for an hour, or until the fruit bubbles and the topping is golden brown. Serve warm with ice cream. Enjoy!

Serves 8 to 10

simple cheesecake

ingredients

Cheesecake batter:

3 (8-ounce) packages cream cheese, room
   temperature

1 cup sugar

3 large eggs, room temperature

1 large egg yolk, room temperature

1 teaspoon pure vanilla extract

1 teaspoon salt

2 tablespoons flour

1 lemon, zested

¾ cup sour cream

Traditional graham cracker crust:

2 cups graham cracker crumbs

4 tablespoons butter, melted

2 teaspoons granulated sugar

Preheat oven to 425°F. In a medium bowl, combine graham cracker crumbs, melted butter, and sugar and mix well. Grease a 9- or 10-inch springform pan with cooking spray and pour in crumb mixture. Using your hands, press the crumbs into a firm crust. Bake for 10 to 15 minutes until crust gets golden brown. Remove and set aside to cool.

> " *This is one cake you can make many varieties of. Pumpkin during the fall, peppermint during the holidays, lemon in the spring, cherry or blueberry for the summer. Or even better just make it plain vanilla. This is the way my family prefers it with fresh strawberry topping and a dab of whipped cream.* "

In a large mixer bowl, add softened cream cheese. Use paddle attachment for creaming. Beat on medium speed for 4 or 5 minutes. Once smooth add ¼ cup of sugar at a time to cream cheese. Now add one egg at a time. Once all eggs are incorporated, add your vanilla, salt, flour, and lemon zest. Fold in the sour cream. This is the time to add to the batter a filling or flavors. Scrape the sides of the bowl and beat until fluffy.

Pour batter on top of baked graham cracker crust and spread evenly. Tap the bottom of the pan a few times to get all the bubbles out. Put the cheesecake in a sheet pan on the middle shelf of the oven. Fill the base of the sheet pan with water. A water bath helps the cake cook evenly. Bake at 425°F for 15 minutes, then reduce the temperature to 325°F for 30 minutes. Check occasionally to make sure the top doesn't brown. Remove and let cool for 1 hour. Wrap tightly with plastic wrap and store in refrigerator. Serve plain or with your favorite topping. Enjoy!

This batter is vanilla only. You can make variations to it with different flavors and fruit fillings. I recommend the Comstock pie fillings.

Serves 8

roloff farm rustic peach & berry cobbler

2 tablespoons sugar

1 tablespoon cornstarch

½ teaspoon pure vanilla extract

¼ teaspoon cinnamon

4 cups sliced fresh peaches

½ lemon, juiced

2 cups fresh blackberries

1¼ cups all-purpose flour

¾ cup sugar

1½ teaspoons baking powder

½ teaspoon salt

4 tablespoons (butter or shortening)

½ cup milk (buttermilk or heavy cream)

Egg wash with cinnamon

Powdered sugar (for dusting)

Ice cream

Preheat oven to 400°F.

Mix 2 tablespoons sugar, cornstarch, vanilla, and cinnamon in medium saucepan. Stir in sliced peaches and add lemon juice. Cook over medium heat until the mixture thickens and boils. Add blackberries and stir to combine, then remove from heat. Pour the fruit mixture into a 2-quart casserole pan. Set aside to cool.

In a medium mixing bowl, combine flour, ¾ cup sugar, baking powder, and salt. Cut butter or shortening into the dry ingredients until it resembles beach sand. Add milk and stir to combine. Pour spoonfuls of topping over fruit mixture. Bake 20 minutes. While the cobbler is baking, prepare the egg wash by whisking 1 egg and ¼ teaspoon cinnamon until combined. Brush the top of the cobbler with the cinnamon–egg wash mixture. Return to bake another 5 minutes until golden brown. Dust lightly with powdered sugar. Serve warm with ice cream. Enjoy!

Serves 6 to 8

fudgy brownies

½ cup heavy cream

1 cup granulated sugar

1 stick (8 tablespoons) unsalted butter, cut into pieces

1 teaspoon pure vanilla extract

6 ounces fine-quality dark chocolate (not unsweetened), chopped

4 ounces unsweetened chocolate baking squares, chopped

3 large eggs

¾ cup all-purpose flour

½ teaspoon salt

Preheat oven to 350°F. Grease an 8-inch square baking pan with nonstick spray, then dust with sugar to coat, discarding excess sugar.

In a medium saucepan, heat up heavy cream to a slight boil, add sugar and whisk to dissolve, then reduce heat. Add chopped up butter and vanilla, whisk until melted and combined then remove pan from heat. Place chocolate into a glass or metal medium-sized mixing bowl. Pour hot cream and sugar mixture over chocolate and whisk to combine. Stir constantly until all chocolate is melted and mixture is smooth. Cool chocolate mixture for about 5 minutes.

Now whisk in one egg at a time until batter become thicker and glossy. Stir in flour and salt until all dry ingredients are well incorporated. (NOTE: At this point you can add additional ingredients such as chocolate chips, nuts, granulated coffee, or other flavorings.)

Spread brownie batter evenly into the prepared pan, place on middle oven rack, and bake for 20 to 25 minutes. Brownies are done when you insert a knife or toothpick and no crumbs stick. Cool at least one hour before cutting. Serve warm with ice cream or caramel syrup. Enjoy!

Makes 16 to 20 brownies

amy's favorite cookies
EVERYTHING BUT THE KITCHEN SINK

ingredients

2½ cups all-purpose flour

1 teaspoon baking soda

1 teaspoon salt

½ cup oats

1 cup plus 4 tablespoons softened butter

⅔ cup granulated sugar

¾ cup brown sugar, firmly packed

1 teaspoon pure vanilla extract

2 large eggs

3 tablespoons milk

1½ cups semisweet chocolate chips

½ cup sweetened shredded coconut, toasted

½ cup pecans or walnuts, toasted

½ cup dried cranberries, optional

Preheat over 375°F. Combine flour, baking soda, salt, and oats in small bowl. In a large electric mixer bowl, beat butter, sugars, vanilla, and milk. Beat until creamy. Add eggs, one at a time, and beat into sugar mixture at medium to high speed. Gradually add flour mixture until thoroughly combined. Fold in chips, coconut, nuts, and dried cranberries (if using).

Drop rounded tablespoons of batter onto ungreased baking sheets. Cook until just firm or lightly browned, about 10 to 12 minutes. Enjoy!

Makes 3 dozen

There is so much in this cookie, which is just the way I like them. You can really add whatever you desire. As long as you have dough that holds it together, be adventurous. These are my absolute favorites. I like my cookies baked with a little crunch but still soft inside.

kids corner

As parents, we are often thrilled if a tradition or activity rubs off on our children. It's even better when we share something we love and are able to do it with them. That's what Kids Corner is for me. When I began cooking with my kids, we had fun. It was a great way to connect, and now that they are older, they are cooking on their own. It started when I cooked with them as young children. Whether it was our family recipe for jam, or enchiladas, or whatever—it was great to be cooking with my kids. I love it when my Molly looks at recipes and then goes on cooking and baking sprees. We often make things to take to school. We started with homemade chocolate chip cookies, or pancakes on a Saturday morning, and most definitely pizza when their friends spent the night. This was extra fun because each kid would make their own pizza with custom toppings.

For me, cooking with my kids is a special moment spent talking and sharing something I love to do. Now it's a little different with my Jeremy away at college cooking for himself, Molly in the kitchen baking, Zachary still loving mom's home cooking, and even Jacob strolls in when the aromas waft up to his room. I am just glad I put the time in early to share something I love with my children, so that one day they may pass it on to their children. Short and simply, Kids Corner connects you and your children with easy-to-make kid friendly recipes.

banana chocolate pops

¼ cup finely chopped, lightly salted peanuts

Sprinkles (or any other desired decorations)

9 ounces semisweet chocolate chips (or good quality dark chocolate, chopped)

6 medium, ripe but firm, bananas

12 wooden craft sticks

1 tablespoon cooking oil

Place the peanuts and sprinkles in separate shallow dishes or on plates.

Into a double boiler or in a medium heatproof bowl over slightly simmering water, add oil and chocolate. Use the lowest possible heat, stirring frequently, to melt the chocolate. (Be sure not to allow the water to touch the bottom of pan containing the chocolate.) Once melted and smooth, allow chocolate to cool slightly and set aside.

Prepare a baking sheet with wax or parchment paper.

Peel bananas, then cut each banana in half in the middle. Insert a craft stick in cut end of each half. Tilt bowl containing chocolate and dip each banana in, turning it to coat completely. After coated with chocolate, remove and immediately roll the banana pop in peanuts or sprinkles.

Let stand until chocolate sets up. Serve immediately or wrap individually in plastic wrap or waxed paper and freeze for up to 2 weeks. Enjoy!

Makes 12

chicken fingers
& melon

ingredients

1 pound chicken tenderloins

¼ cup olive oil

½ teaspoon each, salt and pepper

1 cup milk (or buttermilk)

2 cups panko crumbs

½ cup olive oil

1 half orange

Your kid's favorite dipping sauce

1 half cantaloupe

20 wooden skewers

In a shallow dish, add chicken tenderloins, ¼ cup olive oil, salt, and pepper. Toss to coat.

In another shallow dish, add buttermilk, and on a plate, add panko crumbs. Prep a cookie sheet next to your dredging station to place your breaded tenders. With your left hand, add a chicken tender to the buttermilk to coat, and with the same hand place it into the panko crumbs. With your right hand cover the tender completely with panko crumbs. Place the coated tender on the baking sheet. Repeat this step until all tenders are dredged.

Heat a shallow sauté pan over medium high with ½ cup of olive oil to about 375°F . Shallow fry each tender until golden brown and cooked thoroughly. Turn the golden tenders onto a cookie sheet with paper towels to drain.

Cut orange in half and remove the inside completely. Fill the orange peel half with your dipping sauce of choice. Remove seeds from the center of the cantaloupe half and place orange half with dipping sauce inside the cavity. Skewer each tender and place it vertically into the halved cantaloupe. Enjoy!

Serves 4 to 6

bread sticks

ingredients

¼ cup (½ stick) butter (or margarine)

1 tablespoon olive oil

3 cups all-purpose flour

1 teaspoon salt

2 tablespoons baking powder

1 cup milk

Preheat oven to 425°F. Place butter and oil in 9 by 13-inch pan. Put in oven so butter melts as the oven heats up. Be careful not to let it burn.

In a medium bowl, stir dry ingredients together and gradually add milk, stirring until dough forms and leaves sides of bowl. Stir just until the dry and wet ingredients are incorporated. Try not to overmix! Add a little more milk if dough is too dry. Knead dough, about 5 to 6 times until it is tacky and can be rolled out. Place dough on floured countertop and roll out into 9 by 13-inch rectangle. Lay dough in preheated 9 by 13-inch pan, atop the melted butter/oil. Cut into ½-inch strips. Bake in oven for 20 minutes. Remove and serve. Enjoy!

Variations:

Brush top with melted butter, garlic, and chopped fresh parsley before baking.

You can also add cheese and garlic into the dough and brush tops with butter and Parmesan cheese. Serve with pizza sauce or other dipping sauces.

For a sweet treat try mixing cinnamon and sugar together and sprinkling on top before baking.

Makes 26

mini pizzas

ingredients

4 to 6 pieces of flat bread
   (ciabatta is a favorite)
Olive oil
1 (16-ounce) jar pizza sauce
2 cups shredded mozzarella cheese
½ cup grated Parmesan cheese

1 (8-ounce) package sliced pepperoni
Italian seasoning (for sprinkling)
½ cup chopped fresh basil

Preheat oven to 425°F. Slice ciabatta rounds in half. Place on a baking sheet. Lightly brush with olive oil and bake until slightly brown. Let cool slightly before topping with pizza ingredients.

On each piece of flat bread, spread several tablespoons of sauce. In a medium bowl, combine mozzarella and Parmesan cheese. Sprinkle each ciabatta piece with a little bit of cheese mixture. Top with sliced pepperoni. Sprinkle each with a little Italian seasoning, basil, and finish with a good amount of cheese on top. Place bread back in oven. Bake at 425°F until cheese is melted, about 10 minutes. Serve with favorite veggies, ranch dressing, or small tossed green salad. Enjoy!

Additional Toppings:
   Sausage, salami, ham, pineapple, onions, leftover chicken, enchilada sauce, Cheddar–colby jack cheese mix, green onions, cilantro, sliced tomatoes, or barbecue sauce.
   The possibilities are endless. This is a great snack for a Friday night sleepover or before a game or practice. Let the kids make their own.

Serves 8 to 12

garlicky fries

3 cloves garlic, minced (or 3 tablespoons prepared minced garlic)

2 tablespoons canola oil

3 large baking potatoes

½ teaspoon each, salt and pepper

Paprika

Preheat oven to 450°F. Heat garlic and oil in small saucepan over medium heat for about 2 minutes. Be careful not to burn the garlic. With small strainer separate garlic and oil and set aside.

Wash, peel, and clean potatoes. Cut in half and then into ¼-inch slices or sticks. In a large bowl, combine garlic oil with potatoes and add salt and pepper; toss to coat. Grease baking sheet with nonstick cooking spray. Spread potatoes into a single layer on the baking sheet. Bake until golden and crisp, about 35 minutes. Remove potatoes from baking sheet and sprinkle with paprika. Serve hot. Enjoy!

Serves 2 to 4

raspberry orange
SMOOTHIE

1 cup orange juice

1 cup raspberries (fresh or frozen)

½ cup plain yogurt

1 cup ice

Granulated sugar, to taste

Combine all ingredients in a blender and process until smooth. Enjoy!

Serves 1

strawberry shortcake
SMOOTHIE

ingredients

2 cups fresh strawberries, sliced and green tops
   removed (or frozen if berries aren't in season)
1 cup crumbled pound cake
1½ cups low-fat milk
1 cup ice
Sugar, to taste

Combine all ingredients a in blender and process until smooth. Top with whipped cream and additional strawberries. Enjoy!

Serves 1

fruity peachy SMOOTHIE

ingredients

2 large ripe bananas, sliced
3 cups sliced frozen peaches, slightly defrosted
1 cup frozen strawberries, slightly defrosted
2 cups peach flavored low-fat yogurt (or strawberry–banana flavored yogurt)
2 cups low-fat milk
Sugar, to taste

Combine all ingredients in a blender and process until smooth; you might have to blend in two batches. Serve with fresh peaches and strawberries. Enjoy!

Serves 2

veggie lettuce cups

ingredients

8 to 10 romaine lettuce leaves
   (or butter lettuce)
1 large Yukon gold potato, peeled
½ teaspoon olive oil
Salt and pepper, to taste
1 large or 2 medium carrots,
   washed and cleaned
1 large zucchini
2 green onions, finely chopped
¼ cup chopped cilantro

½ cup corn kernels, canned,
   (or prepared fresh)
2 Roma tomatoes, seeded and
   thinly sliced

Dressing:
3 tablespoons olive oil
1 teaspoon honey
1 teaspoon mustard
1 lime, zested and juiced
Salt and pepper, to taste

I usually use romaine lettuce. It's easier to handle for kids and not as wide or large as butter lettuce, unless you want to roll them up.

Wash lettuce leaves and lay them out on a serving dish. Cut or tear off the hard rough end off. Slice potato into thin slices. Heat a medium sauté pan with ½ teaspoon olive oil. Add potato slices, and season with salt and pepper. Cook until al dente, not too soft; set aside.

In the meantime, set out several plates or bowls to place veggies in. Using a potato peeler, cut carrots and zucchini into long thin ribbons. In a medium bowl, combine green onions, cilantro, corn, Roma tomatoes, and salt and pepper.

To prepare dressing:

In a small bowl whisk together olive oil, honey, mustard, lime juice, and zest. Add salt and pepper to taste.

To assemble:

On each lettuce leaf, place carrot and zucchini ribbons, potato slices, and top with corn cilantro mixture. Drizzle dressing over each lettuce leaf. Serve on platter or individual plates. Enjoy!

Serves 4 to 6

simple sides

I think side dishes are often overlooked. They can really complement or even make a meal special and complete. I love vegetables, potatoes, rice, and pasta. Even though vegetables are not always my kids favorites—except raw—I've found that roasting veggies really brings out their flavor. Roasting has opened up a whole new world of vegetables to my kids—the world of Brussels sprouts. When I started roasting them several years ago the kids ate them with no turned up noses. Oh, the flavor when you roast veggies; what an array.

Living on our farm for twenty-one years and having several farmers' markets close by, I've had the chance to use a lot of different vegetables that we don't grow in our garden. They have arrived on our dinner table in side dishes and inspired tons of new ideas to prepare them.

Some of the sides in *Short and Simple Family Recipes* can almost be a meal in and of themselves. You can add any of the sides to your favorite salad or meat dish. The Brown Rice Sausage with Dried Fruit goes perfectly with Savory Pork or Simple Fish. You can even pair it with a nice green salad. I had to include my kids' favorites, such as Easy Mashed Potatoes and Baked Mac and Cheese. Both are wonderful additions to almost any meal. Enjoy these Simple Sides. They'll give extra flavor to your main dish.

baked mac & cheese

ingredients

¾ pound elbow macaroni
2 tablespoons butter
¼ cup finely diced onions
2 tablespoons all-purpose flour
½ teaspoon dried parsley flakes
2 cups milk

2 cups grated Cheddar cheese
1 cup grated provolone cheese
Salt
½ teaspoon white pepper (or black pepper)
1 cup bread crumbs, Italian style
Fresh parsley sprigs, for garnish

Preheat oven to 350°F. Boil pasta in hot water, cook until al dente, drain, and set aside. Heat a medium saucepan pan over medium. Add butter and onion. Allow onion to sweat and sauté for 2 to 3 minutes, but do not brown. Add flour and parsley flakes. Stir to create a roux, and cook for another 4 minutes. Once combined, slowly whisk in milk and bring to a simmer for 5 minutes. Now you have the base for your cheese sauce. Add ¾ of all cheeses, reserving the rest for baking. Continue to stir the mixture until all cheese is melted, and your sauce forms.

Just like mashed potatoes, there is nothing like homemade mac and cheese as comfort food. Instead of baked potatoes, try this with hamburgers, meatloaf, a tossed salad, or by itself. You can add chili to this to make chili mac. In the end, my kids enjoy this and, just like biscuits and gravy, it's a hit with their friends too.

Once all the cheese is melted, add precooked elbow macaroni to the cheese sauce. Add salt and white pepper to taste. Stir cheese sauce to coat pasta until well blended. Grease a 9 by 13-inch baking dish with cooking spray. Spoon mac and cheese mixture into the dish. Cover the top with remaining cheese, followed by the bread crumbs. Gently push down on the bread crumbs with your hands to pack them down. Place in the oven and bake for 25 to 30 minutes. Remove and allow to cool for 10 minutes. Plate it up and garnish with fresh parsley sprigs. Enjoy!

Serves 6

roasted veggies

 Most combinations of vegetables work! What does your family like? I like roasted vegetables best. I recently discovered parsnips, a wonderful vegetable. There is a sweetness to parsnips and my kids really like them roasted with carrots. Here are four of my favorite roasted veggie recipes. **99**

CARROTS & PARSNIPS

ingredients

4 large carrots

3 parsnips

1 tablespoon olive oil

1 tablespoon kosher salt

1½ teaspoons freshly ground black pepper

2 tablespoons minced fresh dill (or parsley)

Preheat oven to 425°F. Cut vegetables diagonally into 1-inch slices. Don't cut them too small. Place both carrots and parsnips into a medium mixing bowl. Add olive oil, salt, and pepper, and toss well. Lay out on a baking sheet. Roast for 20 to 30 minutes or until tender, depending on the thickness of the vegetables. Sprinkle with dill and serve hot. Enjoy! *Serves 4 to 5*

BAKED SWEET POTATOES

ingredients

3 medium sweet potatoes, peeled

2 tablespoons olive oil

1 tablespoon light brown sugar

½ teaspoon kosher salt

½ teaspoon freshly ground pepper

Preheat oven to 450°F. Halve sweet potatoes lengthwise and cut each half into about 3 slices. Place on baking sheet and toss with olive oil. Spread into one layer. Sprinkle brown sugar, salt, and pepper on potatoes. Bake for about 15 minutes and then turn over. Bake for another 10 minutes until lightly browned. Sprinkle with salt and serve hot. Enjoy! *Serves 4 to 5*

BRUSSELS SPROUTS

ingredients

2 pounds Brussels sprouts

3 tablespoons olive oil

1 teaspoon minced garlic

½ tablespoon each, salt and pepper

4 slices bacon

¼ cup Parmesan cheese, shavings or grated

½ teaspoon lemon juice

Preheat oven to 450°F. Cut off Brussels sprout ends and then slice in half. In a large shallow dish, toss with olive oil and garlic then sprinkle with salt and pepper. Place cut-side down on baking sheet. Roast in oven for 30 minutes until caramelized and lightly browned.

Meanwhile, cook bacon until crispy. Drain on paper towels. Now remove Brussels sprouts from oven and place in a bowl. Add crumbled bacon, Parmesan cheese, and lemon juice.

Toss to coat and serve. Enjoy! *Serves 4 to 5*

BROCCOLI

ingredients

3 to 4 pounds broccoli

2 tablespoons minced garlic

2 tablespoons olive oil

1 teaspoon salt

½ teaspoon freshly ground black pepper

1 tablespoon olive oil

1 teaspoon lemon zest

1 tablespoon lemon juice

2 tablespoons pine nuts, toasted

¼ cup freshly grated Parmesan cheese (my kids prefer Cheddar)

2 tablespoons chopped fresh basil

Preheat oven to 425°F. Cut broccoli florets from stalks. Cut larger florets in half. Place into a large mixing bowl. Add garlic, 2 tablespoons olive oil, salt, and pepper to broccoli and toss to coat. Spread broccoli, onto a baking sheet. Roast in oven for 20 minutes until tender. Remove and toss with 1 tablespoon olive oil, lemon zest, lemon juice, pine nuts, cheese, and basil. Serve immediately. Enjoy! *Serves 4 to 5*

> *My kids understand and appreciate that I like to try different ways of preparing vegetables and that thrills me. I really like the flavor that roasting brings out in veggies. So many options: tomatoes, zucchini, onions, peppers, butternut squash, and whatever else you like.*

biscuits & gravy

Biscuits:

4 cups all-purpose flour

3 tablespoons baking powder

1 teaspoon baking soda

1 teaspoon salt

12 tablespoons cold butter, cut into small
    pieces

1¼ cups light buttermilk, chilled

½ cup heavy cream, plus more for brushing
    biscuit tops

Freshly ground pepper

Gravy:

2 tablespoons butter

2 tablespoons flour

2 cups whole milk, room temperature

Salt and freshly ground pepper

For the biscuits:

Preheat oven to 450°F. Line a large baking sheet with parchment paper. Combine flour, baking powder, baking soda, and salt in a large bowl. Cut in cold butter using a pastry blender until mixture resembles beach sand. Add buttermilk and cream. Mix gently until the mixture begins to come together.

Scrape dough onto a lightly floured counter. Pat and knead into a 10 by 12-inch rectangle, about ¾ inch thick. Use a 2-inch round cutter to cut out biscuits. Press together the remaining dough and repeat. Place biscuits 2 inches apart on the baking sheet, brush tops with cream, and sprinkle with pepper. Bake until light golden brown, 12 to 15 minutes.

> " *This is one recipe Jacob requests constantly! This kid isn't from the South, but he loves his biscuits and gravy. It's good, down-home comfort cooking. Of course, his brothers and sister are glad he always asks me to make it, and I always oblige. I have to round it off with eggs, good steak, and a salad sometimes to make it healthy.* "

For the gravy:

Melt butter in a medium saucepan over medium heat. Whisk in flour and cook for 1 minute. Slowly whisk in milk. Raise heat to high and whisk until sauce begins to thicken and the raw taste of flour cooks out, about 5 minutes. Lower heat and simmer. Season with salt and pepper to taste. Serve warm over biscuits. An option is to add sausage for biscuits and sausage gravy. Enjoy!

Makes 2 dozen

ROSEMARY roasted potatoes

3 pounds red baby potatoes
½ cup olive oil
4 teaspoons minced garlic
2 teaspoons Italian seasoning
Salt and pepper, to taste

2 tablespoons chopped fresh rosemary, (or
    1 tablespoon dried)
¼ cup butter, cut into small pieces

Preheat oven to 425°F. In a large pot, place red baby potatoes in cold salted water. Bring to a boil, then reduce to a simmer. Boil for 20 minutes, but poke with a knife to check doneness. When done, they should just slide off the knife. Drain potatoes and cool with cold water. Rinse several times, and allow to cool for 10 to 15 minutes.

Quarter all potatoes, but be careful because the potatoes will still be hot. Turn potatoes onto a large baking sheet lined with paper towels to drain moisture. Place potatoes in a large mixing bowl, drizzle olive oil over potatoes, add garlic, Italian seasoning, salt and pepper, chopped rosemary, and butter. Toss potatoes to coat with seasoning. Spread potatoes evenly on baking sheet. Roast in oven for about 25 to 30 minutes until golden brown, turning potatoes at least once or twice while roasting.

Remove from oven and serve with any red meat or poultry dish. This same preparation can be made with other vegetables. After boiling you can always add carrots, onions, or large celery pieces to roast. Enjoy! *Serves 4 to 6*

green beans WITH TOASTED PECANS

¼ cup roughly chopped toasted pecans
2 pounds (approximately 4 cups) fresh green
    beans, washed and trimmed
3 tablespoons butter
1 teaspoon minced garlic
½ teaspoon Italian seasoning

1 orange, zested
1 tablespoon orange juice
Salt and pepper, to taste

Toast pecans in a small sauté pan over medium heat; set aside.

Place beans in a medium saucepan with about 2 to 3 inches of cold water. Bring to a boil and let the beans boil for 3 to 4 minutes, or until tender. Drain beans. Add butter, garlic, Italian seasoning, orange zest, orange juice, and toasted pecans. Toss and sauté for 2 minutes. Season with salt and pepper. Serve warm. Enjoy! *Serves 4 to 6*

easy mashed potatoes

ingredients

8 large russet potatoes
1 tablespoon olive oil
1 head of garlic, roasted
1 teaspoon dried thyme
1 teaspoon dried rosemary
½ cup heavy cream
Salt and pepper, to taste
4 tablespoons butter

Peel and quarter potatoes. Place into a large pot of cold salted water. Bring to a boil. Reduce heat to a simmer to boil potatoes. Check doneness of potatoes with a knife. The potatoes are done when they slip off the end of your knife. Remove from heat and drain potatoes in colander. Return to pot.

In medium saucepan, heat up olive oil, add roasted garlic cloves, thyme, and rosemary. Sauté and crush garlic cloves with the back of a spoon. Add heavy cream and simmer for about 4 minutes to infuse garlic flavor into cream. Remove from heat and pour cream mixture into a blender or food processor; puree until smooth. Return the cream to your pan. Add salt and pepper to taste.

> To me, if you're going to have mashed potatoes, go all out. Mashed potatoes can go with any main dish, either seasoned, as in this recipe, or with gravy. When my kids were younger, they liked helping me mash potatoes with the masher. They felt like they were a part of cooking with Mom. I've always enjoyed having them in the kitchen with me, but the older they got, the less they mashed!

Using your electric mixer's whisk attachment, mix cooked potatoes on low speed to break them up. Once potatoes are broken up, stream in garlic cream mixture and turn up speed to whip potatoes. Once all cream is added, whip on high for a minute. Add butter, salt and pepper to taste, and continue whipping on high speed. If you don't like your potatoes creamy and smooth, do it the old-fashioned way and mash with a potato masher. Enjoy!

Again this is a basic mashed potato recipe. You can always use heated milk instead of cream and use different seasonings. No need to use garlic, thyme, or rosemary. Get creative and make this dish your own!

Note: The Flat Bread Pizza recipe on page 2 includes instructions for roasting a head of garlic.

Serves 4 to 6

brown rice WITH sausage,

TOASTED ALMONDS, & DRIED FRUIT

ingredients

1 pound mild pork sausage

Olive oil

½ medium onion, diced

1 teaspoon minced garlic

1 cup dry brown rice

½ teaspoon dried thyme

2 cups chicken or vegetable stock

½ cup roughly chopped toasted
  slivered almonds

¼ cup roughly chopped dried
  cranberries

¼ cup roughly chopped dried apricots

Salt and black pepper

Flat-leaf parsley, roughly chopped,
  for garnish

I love rice. Be creative. For this recipe, I asked my kids to help me change it up. They asked me to add sausage. They love it. It gives this dish a spicy rich flavor. I love making a one-dish meal, and it's easy to do with rice. It saves time, and you can be flexible. Even if you don't have all the ingredients you think you should, you still can add anything you want.

In medium sauté pan, cook sausage until rendered; set aside. Heat a large saucepan on high, then add olive oil and onion. Sauté onion until translucent. Add garlic and cook for another 2 minutes. Add rice and thyme. Turn heat to medium high and cook for 1 minute to brown, stirring constantly. Add stock and bring to a boil. Cover pan with a lid. Simmer over low heat for 20 to 25 minutes or until rice is tender. Add cooked sausage, almonds, and dried fruit to cooked rice and stir well to combine. Add salt and ground black pepper to taste, and garnish with parsley. Serve hot with chicken or fish dishes.

Remember this is a base recipe for brown rice, so get creative. I add thyme as an aromatic because of its earthy characteristic—it goes well with sausage, chicken, game, or lighter meats, like pork. For fish I use dill, fennel seed, or even cilantro to keep the brown rice lighter. I also replace the dried fruits with citrus zest and citrus juices when serving my rice with fish. Have fun!

Serves 4 to 6

index